GREAT LIVES IN BRIEF

A Series of Biographies

MUTUAL
IN PARVO

HENRY FORD by Roger Burlingame
MAHATMA GANDHI by Vincent Sheean
ALEXANDER DUMAS by André Maurois
HANS CHRISTIAN ANDERSEN by Rumer Godden
CHARLES DARWIN by Ruth Moore
JULIUS CAESAR by Alfred Duggan
GARIBALDI by Denis Mack Smith
ELIZABETH I by Donald Barr Chidsey
NAPOLEON III by Albert Guérard
GILBERT STUART by James Thomas Flexner
NAPOLEON I by Albert Guérard
ROBERT E. LEE by Earl Schenck Miers
GARIBALDI by Denis Mack Smith
WOODROW WILSON by John M. Blum
LOUIS PASTEUR by Pasteur Vallery-Radot
ST. FRANCIS OF ASSISI by E.M. Almedingen

These are
BORZOI BOOKS
Published by Alfred A. Knopf
in New York

GREAT LIVES IN BRIEF
A Series of Biographies

ACCURACY
BREVITY CLARITY
MULTUM
IN PARVO

These are
BORZOI BOOKS
Published by ALFRED A. KNOPF
in New York

ST. FRANCIS OF ASSISI

St. Francis of Assisi

A GREAT LIFE IN BRIEF

BY

E. M. Almedingen

New York ALFRED A. KNOPF 1967

Sᴛ. Fʀᴀɴᴄɪs ᴏF Assɪsɪ *by E. M. Almedingen*

THIS IS A BORZOI BOOK
PUBLISHED BY ALFRED A. KNOPF, INC.

FIRST EDITION
© *Copyright 1967 by E. M. Almedingen*

I dedicate this little book

to my two very dear companions,

Kathleen E. Dickins and F. M. Pilkington,

whose signature the little Umbrian would have

recognized as his own.

AUTHOR'S NOTE

THE BOOK does not pretend to be a full-scale biography of St. Francis. It does not aim to give minute details of every event in his life. Its primary purpose is to bring St. Francis into alignment with needs and demands which do not change with the passing of centuries, the need for understanding, compassion, and love, and the demand for the recognition of human dignity. Insofar as in him lay, Francis answered those needs in his own day, the whole of his behavior bent on narrowing the barrier between the visible and the invisible but never at the expense of making dust of the former. Staunch and devout Catholic that he was, he yet rises above creeds. Sociology did not exist in his day and would have had no meaning for him because he considered the whole of mankind as a family, and that was no matter for an academic discipline but a flame on the hearth of his inmost heart. A poet's intuition led him to understand that man could not live by bread alone, that dreams and raptures were a part of his legitimate portion, and that the inevitable daily stresses should never be allowed to hound man toward the oblivion of beauty.

There lies a touch of the imperishable upon that life. We, thrust into the breathless and all too often frightening drift of our day, need to be reminded that calm can be found even in the heart of a storm.

This study is an attempt to interpret a life whose virtue is unstaled by the passing of more than seven centuries.

E. M. ALMEDINGEN

Brookleaze, near Bath
June 27, 1966

CONTENTS

I	The World He Entered	3
II	The Beginning of Contradictions	18
III	Damascus in Umbria	37
IV	The Dawn	58
V	The Morning	86
VI	The Lady Poverty Enfleshed	101
VII	The First Shadows	116
VIII	The Holy Land	142
IX	The Happy Puritans	162
X	Jerusalem in Umbria	174
XI	The Homecoming	194
XII	One Word More	216
	A Note on Bibliography	227
	Index	*follows page* 229

CONTENTS

ST. FRANCIS OF ASSISI

CHAPTER ONE

THE WORLD HE ENTERED

"*Les Très Riches Heures*" of the Duc de Berry were not in existence when Francis was born, but their compelling colors are echoed in the least circumstance of his environment.

He was just eighteen when the twelfth century came to its close, a century which had throbbed with the thrust and counterthrust of the conflict between Church and State, a century preoccupied with Crusades, the birth of Gothic, the growing interest in medicine and natural sciences, and the revival of concern for and love of classical Latin. That century had watched finely developed intellects at work in Paris, Bologna, Padua, and elsewhere; it had seen the spread of the vernacular in speech and in letters, and had witnessed the growth of cities and the consequent development of the urban outlook, a climate which even thus early hid the seeds of a doom to fall upon feudalism some day.

And, coloring practically every aspect of private and communal life, great waves of curiosity began sweeping over Europe.

Men who lectured on learned themes at the universities certainly fed the minds of a chosen minority, but the common folk of the twelfth century in Europe, whose intellectual life had not even dawned, would have had as much use for an academic subtlety as their own cows and pigs, and they needed different

channels to satisfy their thirst about a great many
things in everyday life. Read they could not. Listen
they could and did. Every market square and every
fair in Europe became, as it were, a rough school in
miniature. Medieval credulity still held its pride of
place, but gradually questions were posed which,
however simple, pointed at a longing for many more
opened windows than were known to the medieval
man. Some questions were answered. Many were not.

Francis was born into what we may call the very
height of medieval flowering. The Church, for all the
humiliations undergone at the hands of the State,
stood supreme. Nonetheless, energies were stirring
among the faithful, particularly in the field of archi-
tecture. Sculptors, painters, masons, and carpenters
were recruited from the ranks of the laity. Under the
vaulted roofs of cathedrals and parish churches,
purely secular interests began weaving their way in
and out across the liturgical pattern. Those dedicated
places were pre-eminently God's houses, but they also
served for halls of justice, repositories of lay treasure,
meeting halls, and granaries. In a sense painfully
immediate to the medieval mind, these buildings were
also sanctuaries. Once within their walls, even a
murderer found protection—not by man's casual pity
but by God's unchanging mercy. If the secular arm
dared to violate a sanctuary, all those concerned
suffered the penalty of excommunication. In her recognition of the right of sanctuary, the Church did not
condone crime as such but left it to the judgment
of God.

Yet there still remained secular courts, and at times
it looked as though the State ultimately would triumph

over the Church. The Emperors Otto I and Henry II pursued their imperialistic policy to the point of keeping all episcopal appointments in their hands, and the thorny problem of investiture led to the formation of two European camps, the discord reaching its peak with the accession of Pope Gregory VII in 1073. He succeeded in bringing a proud emperor to his knees, but the victory did not last. Some fifty years later, the Concordat of Worms, signed by Pope Calixtus II and the Emperor Henry V, created a rather streaky *modus vivendi*, and neither of its architects foresaw the stormy days ahead.

European energies were not wholly canalized in warfare, but there was little peace and no organized protection from violence. The urban development gathered momentum precisely because strongly walled-in cities could offer shelter which was seldom found in the countryside, open to attack from the four points of the compass. Some cities, particularly in Northern Italy and in Germany, early enough began to realize that their further development and the spread of the imperial power were incompatible.

Religious consciousness, whatever its depth, was taken for granted in the matter of observance, but the Church was scourged by many evils—heresy, simony, usury, and concubinage. The monastic ideal, fostered in Europe by St. Benedict in the sixth century, was all but entombed. Abbeys and priories were primarily wealthy landowners. The hardihood of the Rule belonged to the past, and the ancient link between a religious house and "the poor of Christ" was all too often a memory. Reformer after reformer would stand up and dedicate himself to the unreward-

ing task of cleansing that vast Augean stable, but
many of those efforts barely outlived a single generation, nor were they all in accordance with the day's
need. St. Romuald, for one, formed the Order of the
Camaldoli in the Apennines in 1018, and Bruno of
Cologne founded the first Carthusian house near
Grenoble in 1085, but neither the Camaldoli nor the
Carthusians were equipped to deal with the spiritual
sickness of their day, a sickness which, as it were,
stood in need of open air treatment. Both the Camaldoli and the Carthusians escaped the world's tumult,
their own eternal salvation standing well to the foreground.

St. Romuald's ideal was to whittle all communal
ties down to the bone, and his followers, wholly cut
off from the world's concerns, lived in hermitages set
in isolated and inaccessible places. St. Bruno of
Cologne went even further. His monks lived in
separate cells, kept perpetual silence, fed in solitude,
and did not meet one another except in choir. It was
a revival of the pattern adopted by the Desert Fathers,
but what had once answered in Egypt could hardly
do so in Europe eight centuries later. The undeniable
value of purely contemplative life should have been
complemented by pure and dedicated action, and not
much of the latter could be observed in houses of
other religious orders.

Nonetheless, a hidden spiritual hunger lived on,
and, in a sense, the Crusades were responsible for
its deepening.

The movement gave birth to three military religious
orders, the Templars, the Hospitallers, and the Teu-
tonic Knights, whose purpose was to fight the Sara-

cens and to nurse the sick and wounded, but not to
heal the spiritual sickness of Europe. On the other
hand, many knights and their squires returned home,
a strange compulsion in their minds. They had seen
the hills and the waters once familiar to the eyes of
their Lord; they had observed the rugged poverty of
the land which had bred Him, and learned something
of the humble and hard daily pattern virtually unchanged through the centuries. They could not but
make comparisons on their return to Europe. The
wealth of abbeys, the splendor of cathedrals, the
dazzling pomp of great ceremonies, the most shame-
less traffic in holy things—could evangelical simplicities be found in such a world?

In some such way the hunger for a return to
primitive Christianity began to thread its way through
Europe. A rich merchant of Lyons, Peter Waldo,
knew his letters, and had read the Vulgate. Little by
little the Gospel story became a challenge he dared
not ignore. His entire wealth distributed among the
poor, he gathered together a few friends, and they
wandered all over the countryside, begging their
bread and preaching the Gospel. Inevitably, the movement caught on. Waldo had no intention of breaking
away from the Church, yet in her eyes his activities
were stamped with a heretical die. The Third Lateran
Council refused him recognition in 1179, and five
years later Pope Lucius III pronounced excommunication against Waldo and his followers. By that time,
however, "the heresy" had spread across France, over
the Alps into Northern Italy, and even further. Its
adherents were chiefly recruited from among the un-
privileged folk.

But Waldo was not the first to disturb the conscience of Europe. As far back as 1022 a Council at
Orleans had condemned thirteen priests for their open
profession of what appeared to be a revival of ancient
Manicheism. They were known as Cathari. They
taught that all matter was evil, and they waged war
on sex and on property. By the time Francis came to
the age of reason, the Cathari had entrenched themselves in some parts of Germany, right across the
south of France, and had penetrated into Italy.

At the threshold of the thirteenth century the
Western Church stood at the very peak of her power,
and never before had she been so threatened from
within. St. Bernard's words spoken many decades
earlier rang more true than ever, that it was wrong
to say the clergy were as bad as the people because
the clergy were far worse than the people, and the
reiterated fulminations of many papal bulls confirmed
it. The weakness of the Church stemmed from her
strength. The enormous organization involved a cor-
respondingly complicated machinery which, apparently dealing with spiritual matters, was wholly
laicized in its methods. Ecclesiastical courts fought
the least deviation from conformity—not with the
Gospel precepts, but with usages and ordinances
made law by decisions of men. The rapid spread of
Catharism with its wild denunciation of sex, property,
and matter, was—in however corrupt a fashion—an
answer to the Church's preoccupation with temporal
issues in general and her love of wealth in particular.

There were protests flaming out into revolts here
and there. Conversely, there was much inarticulate
acceptance of the imposed pattern since those were

the days of a credulity which may well seem incredible to us.

The tenet that there was no salvation outside the Church remained a truism for many. The death of the body led to a fearful threshold of purgatorial expiation. Its duration and the final outcome on the Day of Doom were believed to depend on the pious generosity of the faithful. Excommunication meant a severance from God and the things of God not only in time but in eternity. The crude landscape of hell so familiar to the common man certainly worked on his imagination and deepened his fear. The God he believed in must above all be propitiated, and the means to bring about that propitiation remained in the hands of the Church. Masses, penances, pilgrimages, benefactions, and testamentary dispositions were the chief instruments believed to assure man of his eternal safety and bliss. "To the glory of the Blessed and undivided Trinity, to the honor of the ever glorious Virgin Mary and the company of saints, and for the salvation of my soul . . ." rang the accustomed testamentary formula. Men and women bequeathed lands, houses, money, jewels, and even clothes and household gear to the Church for the privilege of "joining the angelic choir in singing praises to God unto all eternity." Those unblessed by fortune would hoard their hard-earned coppers for at least a candle or two, or a Mass to be said for their souls. With all her greed and passion for wealth, the Church never denied hope to the poor or despised the very little they could offer.

The medieval credulity was responsible for the spread of traffic in relics. The least trifle once in a

saint's possession was believed to be endowed with
supernatural powers. A relic could assuage sorrow,
heal illness, avert misfortune, and bring happiness.
Inevitably, the popular thirst for possessing such
treasures tempted many unscrupulous people to turn
relic-mongers. They thronged market squares and
annual fairs all over Europe, crying their wares which
never lacked purchasers. Ecclesiastical authorities
might frown on the trade, but even diocesan bans, imprisonment, and fines were powerless to check the
flow. How many sumptuous reliquaries were kept in
churches and cathedrals, their bejeweled lids closed
over mementos of more than doubtful origin? A piece
of St. Joseph's sandal preserved at a French abbey, a
drop of the Virgin's milk worshipped in Northern
Italy, her wedding ring jealously guarded at Pisa, a
pressed flower from the garden at Nazareth, a bit of
St. Peter's net—and even more marvelous—a feather
from Gabriel's wing fallen to the ground at the An-
nunciation! A mere enumeration of such absurdities
would fill a sizable volume, but to the common man
and woman of the day relics were so many tangible
tokens of a link with the invisible. To question their
provenance would have been akin to sacrilege.

Yet, however sullied by dishonorable practices and
vices of many members, including some among the
Vicars of Christ, however ruthless in stemming all in-
dependent thought and action, and cruel in trampling
down heresy, the Church still remained the only
bulwark against the menace of ubiquitous anarchy
and chaos. Many of her courts were cancered by
venality, but she alone could offer protection against
a lord's injustice and a robber's rapacity. However

stained her ministers' hands, they still dispensed the
Bread of life. Within the framework of orthodoxy,
the Church's children enjoyed a liberty no secular
power would have afforded them. The very schools of
Paris and Bologna owed an immense debt to the
scholars of earlier centuries, their minds trained and
enriched in the cloister. And, at the threshold of the
thirteenth century, the Church, fighting heresies on
her right hand and on her left, continued to create
the environment necessary for nurturing men and
women of true saintly promise.

Pope Urban's call to rescue the Holy Places from
the Saracens appealed to all men of good will. The
way to Jerusalem became a road leading to the gateway of a city not built with hands. Knights would
pledge their very last acre of land to defray the expenses of the voyage—such was the fervor stirred by
the first Crusades. But all fervor, burning like a flame,
ends in cold cinders. Little by little, brazenly ignoble
interests gained over the selfless purity of the earlier
intention. By the beginning of the thirteenth century,
the crusading movement had fallen to the level of
political intrigues and rivalries and become a source
of steady income to many who had no more intention
of taking the Cross than having a meal of leather and
iron. Certainly, prostitutes, shipped in great numbers
from Byzantium, Rhodes, and Cyprus, could hardly
be said to make fitting companions for men supposed
to represent "the flower of Christendom."

In St. Francis' day, all pilgrimages were closely
woven into the commercial pattern. A poor man might
be able to undertake a journey to some celebrated
shrine in Europe and even to the Holy Land by

begging his way or by offering menial services to
easier circumstanced pilgrims. Yet the mischances
were so many that very few of those poor travelers
ever returned to their hearth. Wealthy laymen and
important clerics went on pilgrimage, aware that they
would have to loosen their purse strings all along
the way. Little by little in Genoa, Venice, Naples,
Palermo, and Constantinople regular pilgrims' agents
began plying a busy trade. They made fortunes in
chartering ships, buying victuals, and arranging
armed protection for their clients. The religious purpose in polite foreground, pilgrimages became a business, differing but little from the tourist offices of our
own day. Away from Italy, at Cologne, Magdeburg,
Augsburg, and elsewhere, shrewd men of business followed the example of their Italian colleagues and
fixed their terms for a safe crossing of the Alps.

All great issues apart, the daily pulse of Europe
beat to its own measure. According to preachers and
reformers, life on earth was overshadowed by sin and
sorrow, and the fair world of God's making was just
a vale of tears. But the gloomiest sermon could not
chase the sun off the sky, or rob a valley of its
flowers.

There were festivals to gladden everyone's heart—
Christmas, Epiphany, Easter, Pentecost, St. John's
Day, and others, most of them grafted into the
Christian calendar out of the pagan past. All of them,
once religious observances were finished, offered op-
portunities for merrymaking. Cities and villages
would be visited by wandering "rogues and vagabonds," minstrels, storytellers, jugglers, and acrobats.
Church feasts apart, there were the weekly markets

and annual fairs—always crowded with pilgrims and ordinary travelers who brought their tales of miracles, climatic wonders, and monsters seen in other lands. Weddings and funerals offered legitimate excuses for a banquet. Accouchements and illnesses opened the door to relic-mongers. Any venturesome merchant returning from afar was certain to delight the community with a novelty not to be seen in the neighboring shops, be it some cunningly woven stuff from Persia or an unfamiliar seasoning for broiled ham.

Hazards of weather and travel and the chequered political pattern turned all security into a reed apt to splinter at the first breath of mischance. The very lack of such security made for a greater vigor, keener energy, and an ever-expanding sense of wonder, and none of these would be crushed by the calamities of the day. Things were valued because of insecurity. Enjoyment was never taken for granted. God's Providence watched over His people, but it did not choose to prevent the Devil from putting his spoke into any wheel of communal or private life. So they firmly believed, and by that belief they ordered their lives.

A traveler setting northward from Rome, would, once the Campagna was left behind, cross the Tiber a little above Città Castellana, and there see a steep track wandering away from the river bank toward the lowest slopes of the Apennines. Such is the gateway into Francis' country. The landscape changes at the very threshold, and in his day the change must have been even more striking.

The wild, difficult beauty of Umbria, with its

rocky summits, deep ravines, great forests of oak, beech, and pine, innumerable waterfalls and all but hidden valleys threaded by streams, would have been at once awesome and compelling to him. The Apennines he knew from his childhood held sovereignty over the whole country, but their rocky ramparts kept giving place to woods, olive groves, and vineyards. Every valley he wandered in was girdled by rocks, many of them too steep to allow of a foothold, and yet every corner of that landscape seemed to achieve a harmony between gentleness and sternness.

Even the Romans were not able to subjugate the whole of Umbria, and the terrain did not make it particularly easy of access in the day of Francis. Nor were its people close to their neighbors either to the North or the South. In the first book of his *Histories*, Herodotus tells a curious story about some Lydians who after a great famine in their country left it for the coast of Smyrna. Once there, the refugees "built vessels, put all their household gear aboard, and sailed in search of a livelihood elsewhere." They passed many countries and finally reached Umbria in Italy where they settled and live to this day.

The story is supposed to lack historical foundation, and it may well be so. Nevertheless, Umbria has kept a curious imprint found nowhere else in the peninsula, a proud independence possibly molded and fostered by its terrain.

In the Middle Ages, the region had several little communities, each deeply jealous of its honor and identity, so many cities and villages perched across the central and eastern slopes of the Apennines. There was no harsh poverty in Umbria, the rich soil re-

sponding to man's labor, the rivers full of fish, and
the woods teeming with game.

The pagan past, still discernible today, was very
much alive in the thirteenth century. Not a wood, not
a stream but carried its dedication to ancient gods.
The country was at once a revelation and a secret,
twin components of poetry, and Francis, himself a
poet, had a few renowned predecessors to whom
Umbria has spoken in the same accents as it did to
him. One such was Propertius, born *c.* 50 B.C. at
Bevagna, a small hamlet midway between Assisi and
Perugia.

In its very heart, the Umbrian valley widened to
the east and west, with Foligno lying to the south and
the grim walls of Perugia to the north. Sharp to the
east, commanding a distant view of the Adriatic, lay
Assisi, straddling across a spur of the Apennines, a
happily unplanned town of narrow winding streets,
some of them ending at an edge from where the
whole of the valley below could be seen. Those streets
were scented with crushed grapes, olive, garlic, stale
incense, dust, and ordure. The rose-red houses, their
windows rather mean and their stairways steep, were
well-built and stood foursquare to the fierce winds of
late autumn and winter. It was a prosperous town,
and most of the streets had shops, the varied wares
laid out on sloping shelves which jutted out into the
street, all chaffering being done in the open. Assisi
boasted a spacious market square, the bishop's palace,
the cathedral, with the town hall and the jail built
round it. Away from the coil of the streets, halfway
up a steep hill stood the castle of the feudal lord, and
a little further to the east loomed the thickly wooded

Monte Subasio, its lower ranges enameled with wild flowers throughout the three seasons of the year and its peak encircled by the walls of an abbey. The pulse of business beat ceaselessly and urgently in the shops and up and down the market square. The bells of San Rufino and all the other churches told the hours, and the strictly canonical graph of time leant toward eternity.

Yet even twelve centuries of Christianity had not stamped out an older faith which continued whispering to man, woman, and child, here enlarging their hope, there deepening their fear, here again counseling them to keep aloof. Any oak tree in the neighborhood was revered, and mistletoe held in deep affection—even a child aware that it must not be cut except on the first day of the moon's quarter. A merchant would not sign a bill with a salt cellar on the table. Young girls were instructed by their mothers in the virtues of herbs, weeds, vine leaves, and narcissi. Wild flowers at the foot of an oak must never be picked to avoid the displeasure of a deity unnamed in Christian prayers. Never discussed and never explained, the ancient faith lived on.

The loveliness of the Umbrian landscape endured in the face of all the ugliness devised by man. The whole breadth and length of the peninsula were then ravaged by war, anarchy, misery, and tyranny. Pillage, spells of famine, continuous brigandage and pestilence, such were some of the day's flails. Towns, abbeys, and castles must be built on hilltops to ensure some protection against violence. Yet seed was sown, fledglings left their nests, and lambs were born on mountain slopes, harvests of corn, grapes, and olives gathered—year in, year out. The marvelous and orderly business of the seasons came and went, its heartbeat undisturbed by man's stupidity and savagery.

CHAPTER TWO

THE BEGINNING
OF CONTRADICTIONS

AT the end of the twelfth century, in one of the narrow winding streets of Assisi stood a tall house of rose-red stone. It would hardly have been distinguished from its neighbors were it not for a very large opening on the ground floor. After sunset, stout shutters, reinforced by broad bands of iron, protected the opening from "all untoward happening." By day, those wide sloping shelves, which ran down almost to street level, afforded much delight to the women of Assisi. Even on a gray wintry day they would be reminded that the rainbow was part of God's creation, so rich, varied, and colorful were the wares of Piero Bernardone, reputed to be the wealthiest mercer in the whole of Umbria. Bolts of woolen cloth of all colors, rose, saffron, and violet silks, garnet and sapphire velvet, figured brocades and fine linen, lay spread on those shelves, with big silver scissors lying in readiness to satisfy a customer's demand. The stuffs were good, and all in all it was that kind of merchandise which breathed of adventure and romance, and evoked images a poet would have recognized.

But Piero Bernardone had as much use for poetry as his sumpter mules which carried his wares across the Alps. A shrewd businessman, he saw his fortune grow rather than diminish and that in spite of the

uneasy political climate of his day. Many people's
loyalties were then divided, and so were Piero's, but
in a cunning manner. He traveled far beyond Umbria
and he met many people. His assent and dissent invariably ran in accord with the hour's environment.
And the climate was uneasy indeed.

The Lombard League, having almost miraculously
routed Frederick Barbarossa's troops at Legnano in
1176, had by the Treaty of Constance wrested many
liberties for the peninsula, but there was not even a
semblance of peace from the Alps down to the southern tip of Calabria. Italy resembled a patchwork
quilt, its colors quarreling one with another. Milan,
Genoa, and Venice spoke a language not always in-
telligible to the people of Tuscany, Umbria, the
Roman Campagna, and Naples. To the great majority,
"Italia" was little more than a word on the lips of
fanatics. Imperial encroachments were resented from
north to south, but all sense of unity was lacking, and
one did not have to be a prophet to see that the hard-
won liberties would not endure.

The ubiquitous unrest did not prevent Bernardone
from enlarging his business horizons. An important
mercer had to travel further than Florence, Lucca,
and Genoa for his wares, and many a time Bernardone crossed the Alps—usually chafing at the expense.
These journeys cost dear; the day's hazards made it
imperative for a number of armed men to accompany
the merchant, and such men could not be hired for
nothing, nor were their weapons particularly cheap.
But, for all the grumbling, Bernardone knew that
the results of his expeditions would more than repay
the cost.

The map of the day's textile industry was clearly
etched in his mind. He knew that the finest woolen
cloths came from the Low Countries and German
cities, and that the great harbor of Marseilles gave
anchorage to ships from Egypt, their cargo the best
flax to be found anywhere. From Syrian merchants
he would buy the finest cotton for the European market. Cotton was also grown in Apulia, but the stuff
woven from it was of too poor a quality to engage
Piero's interest. He served many noble families and
always bought of the very best—gorgeously colored
velvets from Lyons and cunningly figured brocades
from Byzantium and Persia.

Nor was his business limited to a mercer's trade.
Bernardone so arranged his affairs that he had always
funds available for approved borrowers, the rate of
interest as high as he dared fix it.

Wealth and social aggrandizement were twin
beacons on his sky. No merchant's daughter in Assisi
was good enough for him to marry. Yet he knew it
was useless to hope for an alliance with some noble
family. So once he came back from the Alps, bringing a French bride to his house. Her dowry was not
great, but she certainly brought better blood than her
husband could boast of. Mona Pica was a knight's
daughter from Provence.

About 1182 Bernardone returned from another expedition and learned of a son's birth—given the names
of Giovanni-Francesco at the font of San Rufino. The
first choice was Mona Pica's, but Piero preferred the
second name from the beginning.

Of Francis' earliest years even the most inventive
hagiographers cannot say much. Certainly, he was

not a beautiful child. We know nothing of his early ailments but, to judge by later evidence, Francis could never have been very robust. We know that a priest of San Giorgio taught him his alphabet, sums, and a little Latin. Writing was acquired slowly and painfully, and to the end of his life Francis would not be at ease with a pen in his hand. Because of Mona Pica, the boy was bilingual, and early enough learned French songs and romances, the story of Roland enflaming his imagination. In common with all other children of the day, he spent most of his time out of doors—either in the streets and squares of Assisi, or in the neighboring countryside. The children danced, sang, and played games. Very early they accepted little Bernardone as their leader. He invented most of the games, their common denominator being the involvement of Christian knights against the Saracens. Many travelers came to his father's house, and Francis was spellbound by their stories. Already he dreamed of spurs on his feet and a dedicated sword in his hand.

Small, witty, quick-tempered, he was not handsome, but he had a remarkable voice, soft, sweet, and charged with a peculiarly compelling quality. When he sang French songs learned at his mother's knee, the household was enraptured. Moreover, he walked, danced, and ran with an inherited grace, and a certain quality in him soon caused comment in Assisi. Francis' courtesy suggested that he was a nobleman's son rather than a merchant's. So exquisite were the boy's manners that Bernardone, having visited many great families in France, began dreaming most foolish dreams about the future, and Francis became the embodiment of his father's latest ambition which he took to translating into clumsily obvious terms. Never before known for open-handedness under his roof, Bernardone grudged none of his most expensive wares to his son. When Francis' playmates were invited to a meal, delicacies would appear on the table. When the boy went to amuse himself at a fair, he carried gold in his pouch, and his clearly unreasoned generosity to his friends never angered Bernardone.

When Francis was still a child, Barbarossa's successor, the Emperor Henry VI, took advantage of the internal dissension in Italy and ground to dust all the liberties won by the Lombard League after the Treaty of Constance. Such was the young Emperor's strength that none dared oppose him. In her turn, Assisi forfeited her freedom. Conrad of Schwabia, created Duke of Spoleto, had the city under his mailed fist. The immense gray massif of the ducal castle was perched on a hilltop above the city. Conrad's taxes began to bleed the city white, and there was much rebellious muttering, but Bernardone, having learned the rules of the difficult game, offended neither his feudal lord nor the city, and his prosperity grew from year to year.

Mona Pica bore her husband many more children, but all of them remain in a misty background, and not even their names were recorded for posterity. There was just Francis, who grew in ease and luxury, assured of everyone's affection. His appearance certainly did not justify it. He was small and thin; his features were regular enough but there was nothing particular about them. His eyes were a very ordinary brown, his nose rather small, his chin—most deceptively—hinted at weakness. But he moved with a

grace known to very few, and his voice enchanted his
listeners. It was—even in those early days—a voice to
captivate any listener by its sweetness and harmony.
Presently childish games gave pride of place to more
important public festivities. Assisi might grumble
about the Duke of Spoleto, and the taxes he imposed
certainly weighed heavily, but the wealth of the leading citizens could meet them, and festive occasions
grew in number because of a Duke's close neighborhood. The Duke demanded much—but he gave back
as much as he got. There were tournaments with
horses in housings of violet and crimson velvet, their
feet shod in silver. There were fountains playing
wine turned by sunlight into cascades of liquefied
rubies. There were musical festivals—with lutes playing at every corner and young voices breaking into
Provençal songs first heard at the ducal castle. Pierre
Vidal and many other troubadours were then in Italy,
and their songs of *amour courtois* caught Francis
into their silken web. The delicate themes were at one
with his secret dreams.

> God loves honor and courtesy,
> God hates pride and dishonesty,
> God listens to good prayers—
> Love does not turn them away.

There were also songs by Raimbaut d'Orange, a poet
who died some ten years before Francis was born,
songs of love and of longing for God "who fails in
nothing at all. . . ." "*Mas Dieu, que no faill en re. . . .*"
and Francis learned them all.

Presently, sons of noblemen, some not so well endowed as Bernardone, accepted Francis as their equal, a pleasing fiction since none could match him in courtesy and grace. Bernardone's ambition vaulted higher and higher. Once he watched his son leave for some festive occasion, a cloak of sapphire velvet across his shoulders, an amethyst buckle agleam on his black coat, and his parti-colored hose of French make flashing in the sun. There was no arrogance in Francis but any stranger would certainly have taken him for a lordling, and Bernardone said to himself, "God's ways are beyond comprehension. My son is as good as a duke's son, and why should he not get a duke's daughter for his bride? The more important travelers he meets, the better," and Bernardone astonished his thrifty wife by extending his hospitality more and more. It pleased him to have Francis listen to the guests' talk of bigger cities and their splendors, of marvels witnessed or heard about, of a duke's prowess in the Holy Land, of someone's saintliness, and of chivalry.

Francis did not greatly care about marvels, miracles, and monsters, but the theme of chivalry enraptured him. To him, it stood for a life with the breath of dawn upon it. All its hardihoods and dangers notwithstanding, it held a compulsion as delicate as a butterfly's wing. More hungrily than ever before the boy dreamed of winning a knight's spurs and of dedicating his entire self to the service of some lady—as yet even unnamed in his imagination. The roseate mood would not leave him until a casual remark dropped by one of his companions made it clear to Francis that genuine knightly exploits were beyond the grasp of a merchant's son. The sour words were at once contradicted by another nobly born sprig, but Francis, himself unsure, carried the problem to Bernardone. "Of course, you shall be a knight one day," the mercer said.

His dreams were ambitious but he was not a fool. Francis might be the dandy-in-chief of the city but the father would not allow him to idle whole days away. At certain appointed hours the boy, silver shears in hand, had to attend to his father's business, and Bernardone would not release him from this duty even after hearing about the contemptuous words flung at him: "A knight? But you must be bred in a different way. You work in a shop. And my mother's maids would be beaten hard if they dared to speak to her in the way the servants speak to your mother!"

Francis' own clothes were exquisite, and the mercer decided that he could afford to offer credit to his noble companions. Silks, brocades, and velvets, all unpaid for, were in Bernardone's eyes so many rungs of a ladder for his son to climb, but there were not many social heights to reach in Assisi. Francis should go further north, past Perugia, Florence, and Pisa to Genoa and Milan, there to find wider scope and infinitely more glittering possibilities. Or else southward to Rome, to gain some eminence at the papal court. Who could foretell the color of the future except that it was certain to dazzle everybody's eyes? So Bernardone talked to his wife and his intimates, loosened his purse strings again and again, and plunged deeper and deeper into fantasies.

And so did Francis. To be the king dandy of Assisi no longer satisfied him. Tournaments and other public festivities began to bore him. He looked about for different diversions, and little by little he became the sovereign buffoon of the city, his nobly bred companions eagerly accepting his lead. Contemporary biographers sorrowfully record one deplorable incident after another. Supper eaten and far too much wine drunk, Francis and his boon companions would leave the house for the streets and spend the night in a manner which more than anything enhanced Bernardone's foolishness in pandering to his son's whims. A few of the pranks were dangerous, others unkind and vulgar, and all were senseless. They would pour Bernardone's best wine into the gutters, set fire to a haystack at a farm just outside the city, and reward the indignant owner with a sum ten times above the cost of the damage. They would knock at the doors of respectable citizens and tell them that Assisi was being threatened by a Perugian force. Often enough they had their horses saddled and galloped up and down the narrow twisting streets, shouting and singing at the tops of their voices. To collect a great number of cauldrons and to spend the whole night in the square, hammering away at them, was another of their amusements.

Such buffoonery was in keeping with the temper of the moneyed youth at the time and there was hardly a city in the peninsula which did not suffer from those nightly pranks, but all the hoaxes and worse were certainly out of accord with Francis' manners. Having disturbed everybody's sleep and having damaged the neighbors' property, he would offer most courteous apologies. Those, however, did not make up for a broken night or repair a splintered door.

There were complaints and fines, but Bernardone

was held in awe by the municipality and they had not the courage to act with effective sternness. The mercer could well afford to pay the fines and knew that the prison gates would never open to receive his son. For the rest, Bernardone answered his wife's tears by a shrug. Francis' friends came from nobility, and that justified everything in the eyes of Francis' father.

There is one rather curious point about that part of the chronicle. Later, Francis' pious biographers would spare no efforts to emphasize his "viciousness" during that period. In the Testament written at the very close of his life Francis refers to it all briefly enough: "When I lived in sin. . . ." Moreover, the company he kept at the time certainly lends color to the suggestion that debauchery and profligacy went hand in hand with buffoonery. But the suggestion hangs in mid-air. Neither then nor later was a single girl's name coupled with his. Had there been one such mention, Francis' enemies would certainly have seized their chance to blacken his name still more. It is clear that the leader of Assisian dandies, who spent his father's money like water and idled as much as he dared, kept himself aloof from all erotic dalliance. Francis certainly was in love with life and nature and —possibly—even at that early stage in love with an image vaguely perceived in the Provençal songs he loved to sing, but at the time the image would have remained remote, a faint silver-edged streak all but lost in the hyacinth distance.

That particular phase ended as abruptly as it had started.

Francis was about sixteen when Lotario de' Conti

di Segni, though not yet in priestly order, was elected
Pope under the name of Innocent III, and the German influence in Italy suffered an immediate shock.
Hopes for a weakened imperial yoke began stirring
up and down the peninsula. Year by year, more and
more ancient rights came to be remembered. In 1202,
Assisi took the law into its own hands. The populace
sacked the ducal castle, and Conrad of Schwabia became a refugee in the neighboring stronghold of
Narni. With the tyrant gone from among them, the
Assisians decided to protect themselves from all future aggression by building high walls to encircle
"the liberty."

It was a sensible enough measure, but the sack of
the castle left the populace in a mood of discontent.
They had had their will of one rich man's treasure,
but there remained the wealthy burghers and clerics
in Assisi, whose great possessions could not but tease
the poor folks' minds and there were many poor
in the town. In the end, bands of hungry have-nots
rose in revolt against the haves, and a civil war broke
out in the city. At that very moment, Perugia, always
a difficult and dangerous neighbor, chose a feather-
weight pretext to declare war on Assisi.

The home quarrel instantly forgotten, the Assisians
—and Francis among them—went out to meet the
enemy and were immediately routed. Together with a
great many others, young Bernardone was captured
and carried away to Perugia.

Piero Bernardone had spared nothing to equip his
son for the battle, but no gold could have purchased a
knight's cognizances for Francis. His armor and
money appropriated by the captors, the most elegant

young man of Assisi was thrown into a dank dungeon, iron chains on his wrists and ankles, and a filthy straw pallet for his bed. For the rest, there were oaths and blows from the guards, mildewed bread, tepid water, and stale fish for the daily diet, and the none too cheerful companionship of other captives convinced that they would be forgotten by their kin and left to die in prison. There was no talk about any ransom in the dungeon since none among them—Francis excepted—had enough substance to arrange their release.

From the first day he refused to share their misery. There were no comforts, no sky to look at and no birdsong for him to hear, but he knew many songs by heart, and he sang them. Accustomed to delicate meals served in luxury, he ate the revolting provender with gusto. Used to soft scented bedding, he did not grumble about the dirty straw, nor did he weep over the privations and indignities. The Perugians, hearing him sing, laughed at him for a fool. The other prisoners grew more and more indignant at what they took to be lack of sensibility. Some insisted that he was mad. Others said that his extraordinary behavior was a pose adopted to curry favor with the guards. All cursed him for his gaiety which, as they dimly sensed, seemed to dwarf their own right to complain.

Their curses were so much spent breath to Francis. He went on singing, speaking courteously, and giving his services to the sick among the prisoners.

"You have certainly lost what poor wits you were born with," a man once shouted at him. Francis smiled, bowed, and replied:

"You may well be right, but the time will come

when the whole world will pay me homage," and, bowing again, he broke out into a gay Provençal song.

Such a fantastic claim at once confirmed the general opinion that the harsh captivity had more than crippled Francis' brain. The strange words would be duly recorded by the biographers. Francis may or may not have spoken them. However prophetic, they are certainly arrogant and seem to echo his wild moods on the eve of the Perugian campaign.

His imprisonment lasted a year. In the end, the delicate flesh triumphed over the spirit, and Francis fell a victim to a fever engendered all too easily in those conditions. His companions, however irritated by him, were not quite heartless and did not deny what few services they could offer, but Francis was a very sick man when he returned to Mona Pica's care. Once again Piero grudged nothing. The finest medical skill within reach was called upon, and Francis recovered. But Mona Pica went on fussing with her simples and cordials—so thin, pale, and listless did her son look when, leaning on a stick, he began ambling from one room to another.

It was spring. The pale roseate foam of almond blossom turned Assisi into a faery city. The lower slopes of Monte Subasio lay lavishly carpeted with tiny wild narcissi and primroses. Beeches trembled to faint green-gold, and birdsong broke from every tree. The Umbrian valley breathed with praise from end to end.

From early childhood Francis had loved the season. In his late teens he had composed some rhymes in its honor. But that year of 1203, neither the stirring sap nor the triumphant color had any language for him. All the delights were gone. He would stare at the posies of wild flowers arranged by his mother, and they seemed so many bunches of rank weeds. He moved about, a shadow among shadows.

His parents saw the gray listlessness but it did not disturb them. A whole year spent in a filthy prison, a grave illness—what else could anyone expect?

One morning Francis left the house for the first time since his return from Perugia. He made for Porta Nuova, the city gate nearest to his home. He longed for a glimpse of the countryside, dimly hoping that it would put an end to the strange deadness within him.

Once outside the city, Francis took the twisting road to Foligno. To the left towered Monte Subasio, its gaily beflowered slopes having the thick woods of pine and oak for their background, with the tall abbey walls at the very summit. To the extreme right, a range of hills ran steeply northward, their umbrella pines, cedars, and tamarisks vanishing in the lilac-blue distance. Presently, the curving road narrowed to lose itself in a valley threaded by countless streams, their music mingling with birdsong.

That world, familiar to Francis since his earliest years, kept its loveliness all through the seasons, but in April it became a song—from the topmost frond of a fir to the humblest blade of young grass. Yet on that morning he looked at it and saw none of the beauty. Even the music of running water and the song of a lark overhead could not reach him. He sat down under the shade of an old cedar and buried his face in both hands.

He could understand neither himself nor the world he lived in. For the first time in his life he knew he was standing all alone, cut off from hope and joy, and condemned to a never-ending uselessness. He sat very still, his eyes closed against all the glad evidence of a spring morning.

He was frightened of his loneliness, and there seemed no remedy for his fear. He felt ashamed of his uselessness but even his shame seemed part of the same uselessness; it did not make him see a single task he could shoulder.

Francis was a child of his generation. Baptized and confirmed, he knew enough Latin to follow the Mass and a few of the Church offices, Vespers in particular. Waves of heresies then sweeping over France, Germany, and Italy had not beaten against his parents' door. Piero Bernardone's religion was largely a matter of pious surfaces, but Mona Pica certainly knew what real prayer meant. Francis was an orthodox Catholic by practice which had fallen to the level of habit. He believed that the faith he professed in common with all his people was the only faith fit to be embraced by a Christian. He also believed that it was a Christian's duty to wage war against all heretics and infidels. He did not doubt that, his earthly span ended, the pains of purgatory would be his portion to be eased and finally removed by the requiems and prayers and by candles lit on behalf of his soul. It had never occurred to Francis to question what very little of his creed he had been taught, nor to admit that the life led before his Perugian captivity had been in violent disaccord with the precepts of the Gospels. He certainly had a sense of sin, but he hoped that he had been honest in his confessions and that his sins, once absolved, brought him back to God.

Now Francis found himself in a strangely shadowed place, imprisoned within a silence he had not known to exist. Where was the grace of God? Where, ultimately, was God?

There was nobody to tell him that the despair and the feeling of utter lostness were primarily due to his exhausted physical condition, and even more: there was nobody to sign-post the road out of the spiritual wilderness. He would himself sum it all up in a pithily brief phrase in one of his writings. "Nobody showed me. . . ." "*Nemo ostendebat mihi.*"

Francis had never had a spiritual counselor, nor were there many such to be found either in Assisi or in the immediate neighborhood. Both clergy and laity conformed to all the demands made upon them by the Church, but rarely would such conformity carry either depth or height. In broad terms, the ordinary allegiance followed the strict canons of planimetry. All other-worldly matters were subject to the three-dimensional law. Hell could be avoided by good works, fasting, almsgiving, prayers, and Masses, although everything depended on God's ultimate judgment, and nobody could really be certain of gaining eternal bliss. Still, that was the one goal to strive for—the road to Paradise, with St. Peter opening the narrow gate, and the Virgin welcoming a redeemed soul with a smile. And Francis had once heard a traveler say that any crusader, fallen in battle for the honor of God and the Cross, escaped Purgatory and went straight into the presence of God.

Now all of it seemed as misty as a landscape seen

on a morning denied a sunrise. Was something being asked of him? What was it, and by whom was it asked?

Yet that early sense of total lostness began losing its sharpness as Francis went on gaining in strength. Spring deepened into the reckless richness of summer, and he again experienced the joy he had known before. Little by little, as his companions sought him out and begged him to return to his former occupations, Francis again grew possessed by dreams of glory—with not a breath of any spiritual objective. It is true that on occasions he would be seized with a vague sense of dissatisfaction, but he brushed it aside, and there was no one to help him nurse those first seeds of genuine spiritual awakening. There was no priest who would have understood him, and his friends would have wondered if his wits had been really affected by the long imprisonment.

So the ambition grew in shape and clarity. A mercer's son, Francis was more determined than ever to win a knight's spurs. Those were easy enough matters to discuss with his father and his boon companions. Again Piero's hope soared on wings. And the friends took to assuring Francis that, all his qualities considered, knighthood would indeed come within his reach—one day.

Francis had no doubts that it would and, presently, to the great joy of the family, chance came his way. A few nobles of Assisi, Narni, and Foligno decided to band together and go to Apulia to join Gautier de Brienne who, in Pope Innocent's service, was fighting a revolt against the Holy See. De Brienne's name stood for the embodiment of true knighthood, and when a friend getting ready to set out suggested that he could arrange for Francis to join the expedition as a knight's squire, the young man could hardly believe his good fortune.

Piero did. Though busy with many preparations for his own imminent departure for France, the mercer threw himself wholly into the business of getting his son ready. He loosened his purse strings to such an extent that Francis' equipment soon roused the envy of his companions. They said they had seldom seen a dedicated knight provided with such sumptuous gear and such thoroughbred horses, but Piero merely shrugged and replied that even a humble squire need not go shabby if his father could afford to supply him with a trifle or two.

At last, after a solemn Mass at San Rufino and the Bishop's blessing, the expedition left Assisi for the south. Bernardone and his wife wept for joy as they watched their son ride through the gates. "Were the Pope to see our son and to hear him speak, he would surely bestow the Golden Rose on him," said Bernardone.

The first halt was made at Spoleto. In the evening of the same day, when his companions were carousing at the inn, Francis left them abruptly. In the night, high fever gripped him. At dawn, the knights, their squires, and servants rode southward, leaving Francis to the innkeeper's care.

The very next day, the fever still upon him, Francis knew he had no wish to rejoin his companions. All enthusiasm was embered. The matter of the Apulian revolt and the honor of serving under de Brienne's banner no longer concerned him. To win a

knight's spurs seemed as futile as pouring water
through a sieve.

Francis was twenty-three at the time. Having
gained a little strength, he left Spoleto for Assisi. He
had no plans for the future.

CHAPTER THREE

DAMASCUS IN UMBRIA

WHAT happened at the inn at Spoleto remains a matter for conjecture. It is one of the corners of the Franciscan chronicle where differing colors all but cancel one another out. The early biographers' insistence upon Francis' having seen a "vision" that very first evening of the journey is little more than a graceful bow made to traditional piety. Any important and apparently inexplicable decision had to be explained by supernatural intervention. But in this case even piety had to constrain itself in the matter of details. The vision might have been of the Virgin, or an angel, or of some saint. A message or a definite command might have been given. The biographers say nothing at all except that he had seen "a vision." The only person who could have lightened the obscurity was Francis himself, and he kept silent.

It may well have been a dream embodying all his earlier longings for a beauty he had no name for, or else an intensification of the mood fallen on him soon after his convalescence. We cannot tell. What is certain is the lack of any definiteness in the experience: it did not bring Francis to a threshold but rather left him at a crossroad.

Piero was away from home when his son returned— to his mother's deep distress and his friends' amazement. Francis' courtesy unimpaired, he had the air of someone who, on waking from a deep sleep, kept

the shards of an incommunicable dream in his
thoughts. He said he had had fever, and certainly he
looked far from well, his face ashen and his eyes
sunken. But he explained nothing at all. Piero, returning to Assisi, burst into anger when he realized that
the dream of gilded glory to break upon the family
would never be fulfilled under the banner of Sieur
de Brienne. What made Francis return, he flung
again and again at his son, who made no reply.
Piero went on probing and more vehemently. What
had happened to all the expensive accoutrement and
the horses? That proved a far easier question to
answer—though the reply deepened the mercer's fury.
"There was a poor knight in need of the gear, and I
gave it to him." Mona Pica begged her husband to
be patient. "The boy has again been ill. Let us wait."

They had not very long to wait. Francis recovered
soon enough, and all the languor left him. His friends,
having first mocked at his return, now decided to
celebrate it in their customary manner by giving a
sumptuous banquet, with young Bernardone as the
guest of honor. To his parents' somewhat qualified
pleasure, Francis did not refuse the invitation and
even suggested that, once eating and drinking were
over, the party should continue with pranks carried
out in the streets of Assisi. "He has not changed at
all," they said when they heard of Francis summoning a tailor and his apprentice to the house and
having his wardrobe replenished more splendidly than
ever before. Once again, Piero did not grudge the expense. The Apulian venture may have ended in an
inexplicable stalemate, but it was something to have
his son once again surrounded by the nobly born
sprigs of Assisi.

It proved an interlude—as brilliant, swift, and abrupt as the flight of a kingfisher across a stream.

Again Francis rode a magnificent horse, danced, played the lute, sang gay Provençal songs, took the lead in graceless escapades, entertained at his father's house, and held everyone spellbound by his charm, wit, gaiety, and courtesy. But he never mentioned the expedition to Apulia. He never spoke about his ambition to become a knight. Each day's brightly colored futilities seemed to absorb him utterly.

But for such a short time! Soon enough his friends were compelled to take note of a certain absent-mindedness and aloofness in Francis. A supper half-eaten or a song half-sung, he would rise and leave his guests, an exquisitely worded apology on his lips. They could not tell where he went on leaving their company but they dimly felt that they would not reach him even if they found him. Mona Pica came to hear of those sudden withdrawals, and felt at once relieved and troubled. Had her son a call to the cloister? Certainly he had qualities, and one day such great wealth would be his that any abbey would be glad to receive him. The mother watched narrowly, reluctant to mention the matter even to her husband. Soon she knew that there were no signs of any enhanced piety.

If Mona Pica had asked questions, Francis would not have been able to answer them. He was at once himself and another. He knew already that something was expected of him, but he knew no more.

Those strange withdrawals became more and more frequent. Francis began spending whole days with a companion who had nothing in common with his elegant friends, a certain Bombarone from Beviglia, a hamlet a little to the northwest of Assisi. Nobody

knew where Francis first met him. Bombarone earned
his livelihood by repairing carts. He had no social
standing at all but he had many natural gifts, and
he soon came to learn that all too often speech did
not accord with his companion's need. They went on
many long rambles together, and sometimes Francis
went to Beviglia and helped his friend at his work.

Those frequent absences bewildered Mona Pica.
She heard about many hours spent by him in solitude
in a grotto all but lost in the heart of an olive grove.
Had he, then, a call to a hermit's life? She asked, and
Francis told her he did not know, and she had no wish
to probe but she was afraid. She almost imagined
her son enmeshed in some heretical web of the day.
There were so many heresies, and some of them
had already breached the walls of Assisi. There were
the followers of Peter Waldo excommunicated for
preaching the Gospel and calling on the hierarchy to
wake from their sleep. There were also the Cathari,
who denounced wealth and condemned sex. They
offered a liberty earlier undreamed of by the majority
of men and women yoked to the wearying daily circumstance. There were also many other deviations
from orthodoxy.

Those were evil days for the Church, and Innocent
III battled furiously against heresy, simony, and concubinage. But ignorance and apathy were also a
cancer, its tentacles spread all over Europe. At Assisi
there was not a priest fit to be anyone's spiritual guide.
Its Bishop, Guido, spent all his energies in quarreling
either with the municipality or with his brethren in
the neighborhood.

Yet there was no cause for Mona Pica to be anxious.

Francis remained remote from all those alien breaths.
He went to Mass at the Cathedral or at San Giorgio,
joined in processions, spent much of his substance on
wax candles, and gave lavish alms. Often enough he
would give up rambling about the countryside, return
to Assisi, and seemingly enjoy his old friends' companionship—for a time.

Once, with Piero away in France, his son decided
to give a banquet at home, and Mona Pica was
pleased to watch his fussiness about the preparations.
He asked for the finest tablecloths, napkins, and plate
to be set out. He decided what wines were to be
offered to his guests, and himself chose the herbs
needed for a special lamb dish. Nothing except his
consummate courtesy kept the cook from losing her
temper when he insisted on watching her prepare a
very delicate fish for the dinner. He put on his most
gorgeous doublet and hose as though he were going
to feast with the Emperor.

But when the hour came, none of his noble friends
appeared. Instead, the house was filled with the lowest
human dregs of the city, the most diseased and
crippled beggars. Francis stood in the doorway and
welcomed them all, and the indignant servants dared
not interfere. The guests swarmed in and fell upon
the food in the manner of wolves tearing their prey
to pieces. They filled the house with stench and
caused untold damage to plates and furniture. In the
end, replete with food and drink, the beggars mocked
Francis for being a prince of fools, and staggered
out of the house to spread the tale of young Bernardone's madness all over the city, while he, suddenly
grave, begged his mother's forgiveness and the serv-

ants' indulgence. As so often before, his courtesy charmed them into forgetting that chaotic day. A rather singular prank, decided the household, and remembered that their master could well afford to make good what damage had been done by "the guests." The city, however, thought differently, and it would not be long before the "singular prank" came to be remembered—in a violent enough manner.

But it was much more than an irresponsible gesture made by someone thirsting for a novel experience. The alms might have been given and the rich food distributed away from Bernardone's house. The episode suggests a fool's motley thrown over the first stirrings of a perfectly genuine inner renewal. It was a clumsy attempt to deny what Francis was still reluctant to accept. It caused deep distress to many outside his own family circle. It lent color to the idea that Francis' brain was crippled.

He heard some of the rumors and swung back to his former pastimes. His perplexed companions were invited to a feast, its splendors to be remembered for many a day in the city. His hair curled and scented, a great jewel gleaming on the breast of his crimson velvet doublet, Francis played the host to perfection, but the banquet had not reached its end when his mood changed. So grave and unhappy did he look that his guests teased him and said that he must have fallen in love, and they clamored to be told the young lady's name. Francis blushed and moved away from the table, but they kept pressing him. At last he admitted that he was indeed in love. A strange light in his eyes, he went on: "I am betrothed to a lady lovelier, wealthier, and purer than any you know," and said no more. The guests protested that they must know her name to drink her health. Francis shook his head. Was it then a secret betrothal, they demanded, and what of his parents' consent? He kept silent. Was the lady an Umbrian? Was she from Provence or some other part of France? No answer came to any of the questions, and the guests turned to their wine, uncomfortably conscious that there must be some truth in the rumors going about the city. Their friend's mind was indeed deranged. In the end, they left the house, unaware that never again would Francis break bread in their company.

The careless, gilded days were over—never to return.

His father was away at the time. Mona Pica may have been told that Francis wished to go on a pilgrimage. There is nothing to tell us except that he left his home so quietly that nobody in the household could say, "He is going," but only "He has gone."

From then on, not even Bombardone accompanied him. Alone, Francis took to wandering about the countryside, often spending his nights in the open and sharing the meals of the field laborers. Time and again he would find his way to San Damiano which nestled against the shoulder of a hill, an unremarked place all but hidden in a thick tangle of olive, pine, and cypress, rosemary and lavender growing about in a splendidly wild profusion. San Damiano had a virtually ruined little chapel neighbored by a tumbledown hut for its priest. In the chapel, a strangely beautiful crucifix of Byzantine workmanship hung over the diminutive altar.

Evidence of neglect was everywhere. The humped

roof had so many holes that bird droppings carpeted
the floor. The tiny windows were so thickly embroidered by cobwebs that scarcely any light came
through. Toads had their habitation in every corner,
and bats hung from the ceiling. The floor, originally
of hard-baked mud, was all too often one puddle of
rainy water. The holes in the roof and a door which
would not shut gave welcome to wind, rain, hail, and
occasional snow.

Many such chapels stood here and there about the
Umbrian countryside, and most were neglected. A
few were still served by priests but some were wholly
abandoned. At San Damiano the priest was old, in-
competent but honest. He continued saying Mass and
Office—but no worshippers found their way to the
all but forgotten chapel still carrying its dedication
to God's glory but unhappily lacking the distinction
of housing an important shrine.

Once Francis had found it, the strange crucifix
compelled him to come again and again.

There he served Mass, and brought the priest what
very modest offerings the old man would accept.
There, too, armed with two besoms made by himself
out of birch twigs, the erstwhile dandy of Assisi
fought a fierce battle against the cobwebs and the
dust. But the disastrously bulging walls remained,
and so did the holes in the roof. Another wintry storm
—they were frequent enough in the Apennines—and
the little chapel would become a mere huddle of
broken stones.

Yet the idea of storms seemed remote within those
walls. Peace was their signature, and the ancient
crucifix, brought by a long-forgotten donor, had a

strange compulsion for Francis. He spent hours on his knees before that small altar. Man's cruelty, having done its worst, seemed a thing of nought, and even the thorny chaplet spoke of glory rather than agony. Francis felt that the gentleness and serenity on the face of Christ possessed the place to the exclusion of all else. His thoughts now clear, now confused, he prayed for a way to be shown to him.

It was at San Damiano that one morning all the darkly clouded uncertainties came to be resolved. None could really tell how the quietening came, but from the record left by those who would hear of it from Francis' own lips, it was something of a paradox in that it fused joy and pain together into a whole.

The Second Person of the Trinity, the Word of God, infinitely exalted and continually worshipped not by man alone but by all the angelic choirs, became an intimate. Having once spoken in Galilee, He now spoke in Umbria.

The book known as *The Three Companions* mentions it with a brevity compelling beyond all known manner of persuasion, "... *ab illa hora vulneratum est cor ejus.* ..." (And from that hour his heart was wounded.)

The heart of the experience remained incommunicable. Francis knelt within those half-ruined walls and he was outside them. It was the hour of Prime and it was also a moment beyond Time. He had always loved light at the rising and setting of the sun. Now it was as though he had been permitted to see a light, its radiance dimming the most splendid sunrise in his memory. Had he been awake or asleep? He could not tell, but he knew that he had been privileged to read the lettering of a love which alone ruled sovereign in time and in eternity.

The words he then heard rang very clear. They were at once a command and an invitation:

Restore My house

The moment, which was no moment in deep reality, came and went. The poor half-ruined walls were all about Francis. The gift he had brought to the priest, some food and a little clothing, still lay on the ground beside him. He knew he was "changed," but he also knew he was back in the world where the dreaming of dreams could not spin a single thread of gossamer on a rosemary bush.

He accepted the command at its lowest, most literal level. He would rebuild San Damiano.

Here, to quote Sabatier, "There are instances of obsession with spiritual beauty, an obsession so absolute that even the ridiculous, not to say hideous concomitants of the realization serve but to enhance the beauty of a perfectly expressed holy idea."

With Francis, the realization was neither "ridiculous" nor "hideous." Rather it was dishonest, the dishonesty all the greater because he was a merchant's son in more than name. For all his hobnobbing with the young nobility of Assisi, Francis was very much at home in his father's business. We know that he accompanied Piero on some of his journeys and that he served his father's customers at Assisi. He well knew the value of the stock and had free access to his father's ledgers.

Now, at San Damiano, with the ineffable moment

gone, Francis said to himself: "The Lord said that I must rebuild His house, and I can do no other."

He left his gifts with the old priest, told him nothing of his plans, and hurried back to Assisi.

Piero happened to be away from home. Francis might have gone to his mother who would certainly have indulged him. Obviously, he had no money of his own at the time. Still, there were presses in his room full of expensive clothes which belonged to him. Finally, there were moneylenders in the city who would have satisfied any demand made by a son of Piero Bernardone. But Francis chose a wholly different way to carry out the command from the Cross.

He reached Assisi, his whole being still tranced by an experience which at once terrified and delighted him. Back at the house, he ordered a servant to saddle the best mount in his father's stable and to fetch a couple of saddlebags. That done, Francis made for the storerooms at the back of the house. Presently, the two saddlebags packed to bursting with bolts of the choicest stuffs in his father's stock, he mounted and rode off to Foligno where, as he knew well, the annual fair was being held. There he sold all the stuffs and the horse as well. Ill-gotten gains in his pouch, Francis trudged back not to Assisi but to San Damiano—there to shake the gold out of the pouch and to say, a smile on his lips:

"Now you can have the chapel rebuilt without delay. The Lord Himself commanded me to do so."

But the old man was so frightened that he would not stoop to pick up the gold. He asked Francis if such a big sum really belonged to him. Unschooled in lying, Francis told the whole story, and the priest refused to accept the money, telling Francis that he must take it back to his father. Francis refused. The old man's fear gave place to anger. "You should never have done such a thing."

The priest was right, but Francis could not see it. In his eyes, the gold belonged neither to his father, nor to San Damiano, but to God. He said so, but the old man would not have it. In the end, Francis picked up the coins and put them on the window sill, the priest remarking that they could stay there—he would never use any of them. Francis, not wishing to return to Assisi, wandered about the woods behind San Damiano. A path brought him to the foot of a steep rocky bluff, where a stream ran close by. His mind confused, Francis followed its course and presently found himself facing a cave. Wild berries grew in profusion on either bank of the brook. With birds and rabbits for company and the music of running water for comfort, Francis stayed there. Sometimes he slept in the cave. Sometimes he spent his nights in the open.

Eventually the old priest found his refuge and brought him what meagre provender there was to spare at San Damiano—a little stale bread and cheese. Francis accepted it gratefully. The old man kept saying that the money must be returned to Bernardone, but Bernardone's son did not reply. The priest asked if he had a call to become a hermit, and Francis could not tell him. "God will show the way," was all he said.

Meanwhile Piero came back to Assisi, and obliging acquaintances lost no time in telling him of the strange happening at Foligno fair. It appeared that

the whole countryside was marveling at it. Piero
heard the rest of the story from the servants. His
best mount gone and so much valuable stock, too!
And the money given to beggars? Everybody thought
that it had been. So from being the leader of the
dandies at Assisi, his son was turned into a common
thief! And where was he? Mona Pica wept and could
not tell him. Neglecting his customers and ledgers,
the mercer took to searching the neighboring countryside, and could not find Francis anywhere. Presently
Piero came to San Damiano, but the old priest would
not betray Francis' whereabouts.

One honeyed summer morning some weeks later,
the city broke into a singular commotion. Piero
Bernardone's son was passing through one of the
gates.

During his seclusion he had grown a raveled beard.
His face and body worn by fasting, his once elegant
clothes dirty and tattered, his hair unkempt and his
feet unshod, Francis looked no different from any
other beggar in the city, but he had hardly passed
through the gates before someone recognized him,
and within a few minutes a crowd was surging
towards him. Men, women, and children had but
one idea in their minds: those rumors about young
Bernardone were true—he had indeed gone mad.

At once the air thickened with jeers and shouts—
"*Ecco, il pazzo, il pazzo. . . .*" Lumps of dry mud
together with cobbles were flung at him, the city's
beggars joining in the tumult with a particular zest.
To the populace of the day, any madman was first
and foremost a source of entertainment but here the
pleasure was heightened by the identity of the mad-

man. Bernardone's son—who had worn rich silks and
velvets and broken bread at the tables of nobles!—
here was a story almost past belief! That would
bring the proud mercer down in the dust, laughed
the crowd, and more stones were hurled at Francis.
Some missed and some did not. His right arm and
shoulder were bleeding, and there was an ugly gash
on his left shin.

The crowd was now a faceless mob and that
summer morning might well have been the end of
Francis' story if the deafening shouts had not brought
Piero out of his house to see that the madman causing
the turmoil was his own son. Piero at once summoned his servants and ordered them to seize Francis
and to drag him into the house. He neither resisted
nor complained. Once he was inside, the doors were
barred and locked. But the crowd would neither dis-
perse nor stop shouting. Mockery was soon replaced
by anger. They refused to be cheated of such entertainment and they might have broken into the house
if the watch had not arrived and sent them packing.
They went, but the market square and all the streets
rang with their deafening jeers. The excitement all
but surpassed the frenzy of the day when they had
sacked the ducal palace up on the hill.

Meanwhile a different tumult had broken out inside
Bernardone's house. Maids were wailing. Mona Pica
was sobbing. Her husband was shouting: "Stop it.
You have given me a thief, a madman, and a heretic
for a son." He turned on Francis and pelted him with
questions, reproaches, accusations. Francis kept silent.
His rage flaming to a peak, Bernardone belabored
him with a stick, and then ordered him to be locked

up in a back room which had no windows, with mildewed bread and tepid water for his sustenance. It was some time before Mona Pica succeeded in obtaining the key to the room. A lantern in hand, she went to minister to her son, and found him perfectly tranquil, a smile playing about his bleeding mouth. He thanked her for her services in the familiar courteous manner. She could not help her tears. All he said was that he had to do what he had to do. As one day succeeded another, the household grew ill at ease. They refused to believe that their young master was out of his senses. Something in his manner at once awed and comforted them. The familiar courtesy was blended with an extraordinary gentleness. Courteous they had always known him to be, but also hot-tempered, imperious, and certainly arrogant. Now there was no trace of haughtiness in him, and a raw country maid on having her hand kissed by him after having done him some small service, declared that he must have been visited by the Madonna in his sleep.

A little later Piero had to leave Assisi for Lucca, and during his absence Francis escaped. According to tradition, Mona Pica released him. He left his home never to enter it again and made for San Damiano to get ready for a pilgrimage to Rome. His mother must have provided him with tidy clothing and some money. On reaching Rome, Francis went straight to St. Peter's and there exchanged his clothes for a beggar's filthy tattered smock, gave away all the coins in his pouch, and then stood motionless, his right hand outstretched, the whole day long. It was the attitude of an accustomed beggar, but everything about Francis, the torn smock notwithstanding, set him apart from the wretched brotherhood of the utterly poor. A few people, passing into the basilica, stopped to stare at him, and then, moved by contempt rather than pity, gave their alms. But the majority dismissed him as a harmless enough lunatic.

They were not quite wrong. Francis did not foam at the mouth, throw fits, or break into a spate of gibberish, but he was wholly possessed. The time spent in the cave near San Damiano and in his father's house had not passed in idle reflections and vain regrets. Francis was still standing at a threshold, but he now had a glimpse of the landscape beyond it.

He was possessed by a desire to love Christ and to spend himself in the service of a Christlike image. An imagination, early nurtured on themes of chivalry, had quickly enough clothed that image into a feminine form. Thus Christlike poverty, seen at its most sublime, became his chosen lady and he her dedicated knight; the poet in Francis was moved to shape these lines:

> Lord Christ, have pity on me and on my Lady
>   Poverty,
> For without her I cannot rest;
> Have pity on her, queen of all virtues,
> Now seated, forsaken, on a dunghill.

The last line may well be taken to sum up Francis' impressions gained during his first visit to Rome. The dazzling splendor of her palaces, churches, and shrines, the incredible wealth enjoyed by so many of her citizens and by prelates, all the evidences of worship paid to gold and to possessions acquired by gold; and—side by side—the crowds of diseased, crippled, despairing beggars, the hungry faces of the tattered women and naked children, all the countless unregarded human dregs creeping out into God's generous sunshine—to beg for bread and all too often be denied it—and then creeping back into the noisome darkness of tumbledown hovels. The wounding contrasts offered by the scene would never leave Francis' memory.

To spend himself utterly became as necessary as air, but the way to that service, even more so its ultimate pattern, remained blurred, so many faint lines drawn by a charcoal stick held in an untutored hand across a piece of virgin canvas.

Francis looked back to the time spent in the cave at San Damiano, and he knew that solitude answered every need of his spirit. Was his way that of a hermit? A life given to pure contemplation in some inaccessible cave, the service to his Maker and to the Lady Poverty expressed in no other terms than those of a refusal to call his own the very rags covering his body? He could not tell. He prayed. He had no answer, but solitude did not cease to attract him.

It happened in 1206, and he was twenty-four years old. The radiance of that morning spent in the chapel at San Damiano now drew near, now receded. Moments of exaltation, serenity, and peace would be followed by darkly clouded moods when uncertainty turned into a deep-biting fang. Francis continued to pray to be delivered from uncertainty, but no deliverance came.

He left Rome, his mind weighed by deep sadness. On his return to Umbria, he chanced to meet a leper

coming towards him. At once the careless profligate
in him stirred to life again. His alms flung on the
ground, Francis ran away, revulsion gripping him.
Yet within a few moments he turned, caught up with
the bewildered leper, knelt in the dust, asked the
man's forgiveness, and kissed the hand which in the
earlier days he would never have touched. Then,
stooping, Francis picked up the coins flung on the
ground, put them into the sore-covered palm, asked
the leper to pray for him, and went on his way,
wondering if he had been a fool.

Francis had not yet crossed the threshold of his
calling. Dishonesty, clumsiness, exaggeration of impulse and gesture, all of it angered most of his contemporaries, and some of it looks anything but
pleasing today. That wildly checkered beginning,
later to be forced into a hagiographical frame,
troubled many who came after, and the painfully
pious records offer little help, if any, in that they
turn a faintly penciled outline into an ugly and obvious daub, and change a poet's approach—as fluent,
eloquent, and varied as a stream—into the wooden
inanity of a mass-produced piece of shoddy statuary.
Yet even at that time, Francis' truth—which he was
not yet able to see himself—was strong enough to
break through the piously imagined causes and effects.

Corn must be ground and grapes crushed to make
bread and wine for saint and sinner alike. Francis
compelled—and still does compel—not in spite of his
exaggerations and blunders but because of them. All
his failings, as it were, serve to greaten his positive
qualities, and all the untidy fragments can be gathered
together to form a wondrous whole where compari-

sons matter as little as a leaf blown by the autumn gusts. Francis cannot be understood if his many imperfections are stripped from him because they have their part to play in proving his truth, and even in his day that truth stood immeasurably higher than the contemporary categories of virtue and vice, of wisdom and foolishness, of prudence and apparent senselessness.

It was during his son's absence from Assisi that Piero decided to turn a family rupture into a legal issue. Some friends had been present at the fair at Foligno and watched Francis sell the cloth and the horse. He had no right to offer them for sale, and the law was certainly on Piero's side. He had the case prepared by a lawyer and took it himself to the magistrates, claiming the money realized from the illegal sale.

The civic fathers of Assisi found themselves facing a quandary when they discovered that the old priest at San Damiano had neither asked for the money nor used any of it. Intact down to the last soldo, the sum was still in his hut, the coins neatly arranged on the window sill. Bernardone might well have gone and collected it. He did not choose to do so. He thirsted for more than gold: he wanted to have Francis publicly humiliated as a revenge for the disgrace that had fallen on the house of Bernardone.

In the end the magistrates decided to extricate themselves from the difficulty by referring the case to Guido, Bishop of Assisi. They felt that since it was no question of mere restitution, the matter should be handled by an ecclesiastical court. By that time Francis was back at San Damiano. Having examined

the documents, the Bishop summoned both father
and son to appear at the palace. To the merchant's
pleasure the Bishop found for him, and Francis was
ordered to return the money. Failure to do so would
mean a long term of imprisonment, a lenient enough
sentence for those days when even a small theft
might mean mutilation or worse.

Piero waited. Such was his hatred for the son he
had once loved that he may well have hoped to hear
that the money had been used or mislaid. But Francis
had it in a pouch. He threw it on the ground and
then and there, in full view of a great crowd in front
of the palace, he began stripping himself, his voice
ringing out over the square: "These clothes are not
mine. They were given to me. Now I tell you all that
I have a Father in Heaven and none other."

The crowd gasped. So did the Bishop, and ordered
a servant to fetch a cloak and put it over Francis. Piero
stared stonily and watched his son bow to the Bishop
and turn towards the square.

Those were the same people who but a short while
ago had mocked at Francis and pelted him with mud
and garbage. Now they stood as still as though his
words had turned them to stone, but many eyes followed him as he went off and those eyes had warmth
in them. The crowd's silence confirmed their anger
against a father using the law against his son.

That father now bent for the pouch and gathered
up his discarded clothing. Someone laughed, and
Bernardone left the square to the hisses and jeers of
the people.

In a certain sense, he vanished from his son's story
on that day. He no longer considered himself Francis'

father; unreasoned affection having given way to vehement hatred, Bernardone would lose no chance of proving his enmity. Both of them stayed on in Umbria, and Francis' links with Assisi would remain unbroken to the end, but there is no record of any further family relationship between father and son. Biographers indeed tell us of casual meetings at street corners and in the great square of Assisi; Francis' efforts at an approach would be repulsed by Bernardone with a curse on his lips.

A successful businessman, Piero was also a fool, his horizons oddly out of accord with his far-flung travels. A wealthy snob, he had been most unwisely generous to Francis only because of a longing to win a corner among the nobility. So Piero, who had never committed a single extravagance himself, would provide for and approve all the escapades of Francis. But the son's ultimate extravagance carried a splendor beyond the father's narrow vision. He disappeared from his son's chronicle in a shamefully dramatic way, the refunded money and discarded clothes clutched in his arms, his respectability torn to shreds by the people's judgment.

Yet it is impossible to condemn him wholly. His meanness and foolishness were certainly great, but he bore an honorable name as a merchant. Unhappily, gold and silver were his counselors-in-chief, and Francis' contempt for possessions branded him as a madman and a heretic in Piero's eyes.

A heretic Francis was not. In the light of the world's contemporary standards he was certainly mad, but his was a madness which reduced the world's sanity to the level of near idiocy.

CHAPTER FOUR

THE DAWN

NOW, though still vague about the future, Francis was happy. The house in an Assisian street would never again be his home, but he had the whole Umbrian valley for his steading. His father had disowned him, but he knew himself encompassed by a love which beggared all comparison. His nights were peaceful enough, his meditations tranquil, his days passed busily. He had not forgotten the command laid upon him, and he begged for stones in the neighborhood. The common folk knew him now for a dispossessed beggar but they did not despise him, and few were the farmers who refused his courteous request "for a stone or two." With his own hands, however slowly, he rebuilt the all but crumbling walls of the chapel at San Damiano and shored up the roof of the priest's hut. One task finished, Francis turned to the leper hospital outside the walls of Assisi. He had no alms to bring to the lepers but day by day he went to nurse them, sing songs to them, and talk about the lovely country so many of them could see no longer. Day by day he schooled himself to carry out more and more repulsive tasks. He would wash the wasted bodies, change the straw for their bedding, and not shrink from sharing the dinner bowl with one or the other of the lepers. When one among them came to his dying, Francis' touch and silent prayer eased the departure.

Not all of them responded. Some were far too sick to care. Others mistrusted a young man who preferred nursing them in the malodorous squalor of the hospital to spending his days in ease and luxury under his father's roof. A few were irritated by his irrepressible gaiety. But none refused his services.

Alms and provender would be brought to the hospital, but occasionally there was not enough, and Francis would then set out for Assisi, a great empty sack over his shoulder, and beg for food in return for any menial job he was offered. The doors of the rich were invariably closed against him, and Piero's sleepless enmity made itself felt at every turn. But the less moneyed folk gave freely, the poor shared their penury with him, and Francis kept none of their offerings for himself. At the beginning, the deep-rooted fastidiousness kept rebelling against such fare, but gradually hunger and humility won the day. Francis would dine and sup off most unsavory broken meats in the manner of one enjoying a king's banquet.

Such, then, was the drift of his days for the next two or three years. He kept his vow to the letter and never touched money again. What services he was able to offer to farmers in the neighborhood would be paid for in food or some article of clothing, and he went on serving his Lady Poverty in various ways suggested by the pattern of life led in the countryside where no farmers were wealthy and where the common laboring folk had taken scarcity for granted since their childhood.

As to the companions of Francis' earlier days, they dismissed him for a madman and a liar. He had

boasted in their presence about being betrothed to
the most beautiful lady in Christendom, and that now
proved to be the most fantastic fable they had ever
heard. Whose lover could Francis be when he trudged
about, unkempt and barefoot, a shepherd's coarse
brown tunic over his body, soiling his hands with
menial tasks, and content to eat pigs' fodder?

At one time elegant clothes, curled hair, and
jewelry would go a long way to redeem Francis' un-
prepossessing appearance, but now, his small body
covered by a ragged tunic, his head continually ex-
posed to the vagaries of the weather, his hands
calloused and roughened by menial tasks, he looked a
beggar indeed. Yet the deep sunken brown eyes
burned with a fire seen but seldom and the gentle
voice belonged to a poet and a singer.

The older money folk of Assisi were full of pity
for Piero, and thought that Francis would end as an
inmate at the lepers' hospital. There could be no other
future for him because he was known to share a
leper's dinner bowl, they said to one another, and
added that his early death would be no great grief
to his kin.

Those few years proved the richest Francis had
ever known. Member of no religious community, dismissed as a fool and a madman, and faintly suspected
of heresy, he was passing through a novitiate far
harder—and in a sense far more fruitful—than any
cloister could give him. He had no counselor to guide
his steps, but he kept going forward, his whole being
responding to the light he had seen. That light
might indeed ebb down to a flicker on occasions and
leave him at the mercy of a midnight mood, not a

star in his sky to reassure him, but even such moods
did not end in retreat. He went on, wholly unconcerned about the future, content to accept each day
as a gift at God's hands, and to do what jobs fell to
his share.

Theology, as such, spoke a language Francis could
not follow, but he sensed that God cared for the whole
world and for him individually. Steadfastly loyal to
the Church, he learned more and more of the shabby
and stained disservices rendered to her by many of
her sons. Clerical greed and ignorance, undisguised
hunger for gold, and brazen contempt for God's poor,
the ceaseless traffic in holy things—such were some
of the wounds on the Church's body—but, however
stained and mottled the surface, to Francis she remained and always would remain the Bride of the
Lord. He rightly held that a priest's sin—however
grievous—could never unhouse the Lord from His
altars or turn other sacraments into hollow mockery.

Francis spoke of it all in his Testament: ". . . the
Lord gave me and He still gives me so great a faith
in priests . . . that even if they persecuted me, I would
have recourse to them . . . I would not preach in their
parishes without their consent. I will not consider
their sins. We ought to revere . . . those who preach
the most holy word of God, and dispense to us spirit
and life."

Busy as he was, the idea of utter solitude kept
teasing him. Sometimes he wondered if he could be
of service to his God only when by himself, castled
within that eloquent silence which heightened his
consciousness of God's presence. On occasions Francis
would be so lost to the surroundings as to take no

notice of a heavy shower. He wondered if the continued communication with his kind would end by creating a gulf between himself and God. He had never been very robust. Now the unaccustomed daily tasks often left him almost too weary for sleep. He permitted his imagination to lose itself in the unbroken tranquility of a hermit's life spent in one or other of the grottos along the wooded slopes of Monte Subasio, with beasts and birds for companions, a stream for music, and great trees befriending and sheltering him. That, surely, would be Paradise on earth, and Francis wondered if in such conditions he could really spend himself in prayer and in service to the Lady Poverty.

Then on St. Matthias' day, February 24, 1209, Francis decided to hear Mass at Portiuncula, a tiny chapel belonging to the monks of Monte Subasio. In common with so many other places, Portiuncula had all but fallen into ruins and Francis had repaired it. It stood in a very secluded spot, and he had loved it from the beginning, dimly conscious that some day he would there hear an answer to many questions. Mass was said very seldom, but he always took care to find out when a priest would be coming down from the abbey at the summit of the mountain.

According to contemporary usage, the day's Gospel came from the tenth chapter of St. Matthew. At the very first words, Francis knew what was being asked of him. Kneeling at the foot of the tiny altar, he followed the familiar words now clothed with a newness and an emphasis he could not escape:

. . . go rather to the lost sheep of the house of Israel. And as ye go, preach, saying, The King-

dom of heaven is at hand. Heal the sick, cleanse
the lepers, raise the dead, cast out devils: freely
ye have received, freely give. Provide neither
gold nor silver, nor brass in your purses. Nor
scrip for your journey, neither two coats, neither
shoes, nor yet staves: for the workman is worthy
of his meat.[1]

The Gospel came to its end. Presently Mass was
over. As once before at San Damiano, Francis' mind
took a swift plunge into the literal. The monk was
still at the altar when the little man from Assisi began throwing away his stick, scrip, and shoes—all
done abruptly and silently, but behind each feverish
gesture lay two years of unceasing inner travail, hesitation, uncertainty. Now all was resolved. From now
on contemplation and activity would be welded together, and the first of the many duties laid upon
him was to go forth and preach.

The Order of Friars Minor was not really born
on that February day in 1209. The least idea of any
organization was remote from Francis' mind. All he
knew was that he had received an unmistakable call
to be articulate about God, Whom he loved, and
about the Lady Poverty. Certainly, he had much to
say. Equally, he had no clear idea of the way to say
it. He was a layman, and in terms of Canon Law, he
had no right to preach. He may or may not have
known it, but even had he known it, the knowledge
would not have influenced his resolve. He held himself
accountable to Christ, and that was an adequate
credential for Francis.

Not for nothing had his first experience been at

[1] A.V., St. Matthew, 10:6–10.

the foot of that old Byzantine crucifix at San Damiano. The story of the Master's Passion had never ceased to compel Francis. The hour in the Upper Room, the vigil at Gethsemane, the drama of Calvary, and finally, the splendors of the Empty Tomb were not just stories for him to read and meditate upon. They were realities to live in, and to Francis they flooded the soul with their darkness and their light together. All their details were just as immediate as the pine needles under his feet. They at once terrified and comforted him, cast him down and lifted him up, and he had lived in that climate not for a fugitively tranced moment but for two whole years. That very day, Francis Bernardone, a layman who had ostensibly forfeited all title to regard and recognition, left the peace of Portiuncula for Assisi—there to stir curiosity, invite much censure and ridicule, and also to compel attention.

He had listened to many sermons at Assisi and elsewhere. The art of preaching had few brilliant exponents in Umbria at that time. There were no pulpits in any Assisian churches. Priests would deliver their sermons either from the altar, or leaning against a pillar in the nave, or even walking to and fro in front of the congregation. They were usually brief. They seldom moved their hearers except insofar as they deepened their fears of the hereafter, since the theme of eternal punishment more often than not stood to the fore.

The day being a feast, no business was done in the city, but crowds were milling up and down the square. Francis' appearance led to loud laughter and jeers, but no hostility was shown, and guffaws died down at his very first words.

All the contemporary records agree that Francis'
voice carried a quality possessed by very few. It lent
a color to the most ordinary words. Strong, clear, and
sweet, it was a poet's voice.

By all accounts, the content of his first sermon was
not particularly original: the love of God, the horror
of sin, the need for repentance, the glory of poverty,
the Last Judgment, everlasting bliss, or unending
torment. Francis' vocabulary was not large, his delivery unmarked by tricks or attitudes, but he had
lived with all he spoke of, and he was enabled to
communicate at least some of his own deep conviction to his hearers.

They certainly listened, both clergy and laity, and
the former hoped that, the sermon over, they would
have an opportunity of declaring young Bernardone
guilty of heresy. They were not able to do so.

That artless sermon might be compared with the
flight of a bird. Properly speaking, it was no sermon
in the technical sense but rather a virgin attempt to
share the joy fallen to his lot. Strangely enough, his
words, born out of and enflamed by personal experience, carried not the smallest sense of self.

Now that hour in the square of Assisi was indeed the Franciscan birthday, not the birthday of a
formally organized Order but that of a tiny fellowship dedicated to God and the Lady Poverty, a band
of men as untroubled by any man-made patterns and
rules as Francis himself.

He had not reached the city gates before three
men caught up with him and said they wished to
lead the life he led. We know their names—Egidio,
Pietro, and Bernardo di Quintavalle, a man of great
substance and many gifts. "Come, once you have

given all your possessions to the poor," Francis replied, and there was no other initiation into the life of poverty. The four men spent the night at Bernardo's house. At dawn they heard Mass at San Niccolò. The service over, Francis went up to the altar, opened the Gospels, and read aloud the verses from St. Matthew's tenth chapter.

"This is what our life is going to be," he told them, and they followed him to Portiuncula and built themselves rough huts close to the little chapel.

But they could not stay there very long. Assisi was at once troubled, excited, and curious, and the news of that first sermon winged its way far and wide over the countryside. It was novel, compelling, and light-shot. It stirred a rich man's conscience out of its sleep and comforted a tired laborer. Little by little, it became evident that Francis' example had set many on fire and Portiuncula became too small to shelter them all. In the end, singing, Francis took his friends to Rivo-Torto, a place about an hour's walk from Assisi, not far from the high road leading south to Rome. Rivo-Torto, once a lepers' hospital, was a more or less habitable ruin. It stood at the foot of a wooded slope of Monte Subasio. At the back of the house, a steep rugged path, edged by a stream, went winding up and up until it ended in the very heart of the forest, in the thick tangle of pine, oak, cedar, and beech, with rosemary and wild vines rioting at their feet. Here, scattered in between the thick trunks of the old trees, were the so-called *carceri*, natural grottos, all most rewardingly in accord with Francis' ideas about a life where contemplation would march shoulder to shoulder with activity.

For a while Rivo-Torto became their harbor, though few of them were there together at the same time.

Here, let his own words in the Testament, written toward the end of his life, speak of that radiant beginning.

When the Lord gave me some brothers no one showed me what I ought to do, but the Almighty Himself made it clear to me that I and the brothers were to live in accordance with the Gospel precepts. I wrote a short and simple Rule, and the Pope confirmed it for me. Those who presented themselves to observe [the Rule] gave all they had to the poor. They were satisfied with a patched tunic, a cord for a girdle, and linen breeches, and we desired to have nothing more. Those in Orders said the Divine Offices. The laymen had the Pater Noster to recite.

From the very beginning, Francis insisted on the necessity of manual labor. To work was the rule of the fellowship. To beg for work assured them of the few necessities they needed. The brothers were not mendicants who shirked work for the sake of comfortably cushioned idleness. Some who joined Francis at the beginning had brought a trade of their own: one was a cobbler, another, a basketmaker, a third, a cooper. The rest offered their labor to farmers in the neighborhood, looking after livestock, helping with the harvest of corn, olive, and grapes, or felling timber. They also nursed lepers and offered their services in what towns they passed through. The only payment they accepted was food. They went bare-headed and unshod, and wore the coarse brown tunics of Umbrian shepherds, a thick hempen cord for their girdle.

There was no ceremony of admission. It was enough for a man to say that he wished to serve God in absolute poverty and to prove his desire by giving up all his possessions, not for the communal use of the fellowship but to the poor, for Francis to call him "brother." Nor was the admission followed by a period of probation. A newcomer would be given what work best answered his abilities. A particular task finished, he would return to Rivo-Torto. There, the customary domesticities apart, the brothers spent their time in much prayer, meditation, and listening to Francis. He taught them much, but he was friend rather than teacher.

The one disciple who in spirit stood closest to him, Brother Leo, recorded many of the master's sayings in *The Mirror of Perfection*.

Francis urged his neophytes:

> Be truly poor, forget the very words "to have" and "to get. . . ." No brother should have anything except the habit he wears. . . . In your troubles or infirmities do not murmur against God or against one another. . . . Let us indeed mourn for our sins but never with an outward show. We must all study to keep gay and cheerful.

Hope and cheerfulness were the keystone of the little community. Despair, as Francis believed, came from the Devil. On one occasion when a newcomer bewailed the sins of a rich man at Foligno, Francis shook his head. "There are some who *seem* to belong to the Devil today and yet tomorrow they may be Christ's."

In truth, those days were his dawn and theirs also. So happy and lighthearted were they that he called them "*joculatores Domini*," and his own gaiety seldom left him.

When away, either laboring or preaching, the brothers slept in barns, haylofts, church porches, or under the open sky. Unkindly weather did not dampen their spirits, nor did frequently short commons darken their day. Contempt and contumely met them often enough, but none of it seemed to have the power to cloud their cheerfulness. Into many a shadowy corner of Umbria they brought courtesy, laughter, and song. Brigands did not threaten them since they carried nothing at all. They wished God's peace to those who drove them off with curses. Merchants, at first suspicious of them, came to realize that the brown-smocked men, who coveted nothing, had not in them to become thieves.

They were men possessed by the love of God, and all their waking moments were molded by the inspiration they received from Francis. Together with him, they were convinced that they had begun their journey toward a city unbuilt with hands. Also together with him, they knew themselves called to invite as many others as they could—not to join the fellowship but to set their feet upon the same road. But, their minds engaged with heavenly matters, they showed no contempt for God's world. They did not consider themselves "exiles in the vale of tears." Rather, they thought they were pilgrims passing through a wondrous world, neither vice nor iniquity strong enough to destroy its loveliness.

Assisi and many other places came to know them well. There was constant amazement, some mockery, much curiosity, and a certain breath of unease— particularly among the clergy who were incapable of understanding the service paid to the Lady Poverty. Francis never expected the entire world to follow him in those steps. But to himself and his men, the least possession ended by possessing the possessor. Christendom was then cancered by various heresies. Was such a bold plunge into the forgotten evangelical simplicities but another departure from orthodoxy? Where was the harm of possessing things when, all the monastic reforms notwithstanding, every religious house had its own treasury and owned land? The clergy watched, wondered, and speculated about the future. The men in brown certainly conformed to all the demands of the Church. They went to Mass, received sacraments, and treated priests with marked reverence, but did such outward conformity serve some hidden and pernicious purposes of their own? The clergy reminded one another about Peter Waldo whose piety could not be doubted. Yet Waldo came to be excommunicated in the end.

There was yet another reason for deepening clerical suspicions.

All through the wild carelessness of his earlier youth, the poet in Francis had paid homage to nature. The feeling took still deeper roots after his conversion when the beauty he saw all around him mirrored the beauty of its Maker. The changing landscape of the skies and the majesty of Umbrian forests, the smiling face of spring and the severity of winter, everything down to the blade of common grass spoke to him of the Creator's boundless generosity to man. It was as though Francis, looking upon "the vale of tears" of stern-lipped theologians, heard its laughter and was constantly refreshed by its song. There was a gaiety and liberty in his approach to nature which seemed utterly alien and therefore dangerous to the ecclesiastical temper of his day. It was an outlook which made one wonder if Hellenic breaths were sweeping over Umbria, and many heresies were known to hark back to the pagan past.

When someone reported that Francis, serving the Lady Poverty, considered himself a wealthy man, suspicion deepened.

His clerical contemporaries cannot really be blamed for the censure. With the exception of Brother Leo, few, if any, among Francis' closest companions came to understand his ideal. They revered it and they followed it. They could do no more. The outside world—and in particular the clergy—could not contain it at all.

The ugly snake of suspicion eventually raised its head. The men now living at Rivo-Torto had once been known by their antecedents and their calling. Who were they now? At Assisi Bishop Guido began voicing his suspicions. The cathedral chapter and other clergy lost no time in lending him their eager support.

"If young Bernardone has a true vocation to serve God," they argued, "why does he not join some religious order? Who has given him permission to masquerade barefoot and in a shepherd's tunic as though it were a habit? How dare he, an unschooled layman as he is, preach about God's love and redemption? And what kind of a vocation can he have? Gravity and recollection are essential to a true religious, and the men of his company laugh and sing at their work instead of keeping silent and weeping over their sins. Anyone would take them for strolling minstrels," said the Umbrian clergy, to whom the ideal of absolute poverty spelt little more than madness and in whose eyes any expression of gaiety in spiritual matters bore the stamp of sinful levity.

The rich laity of Assisi, with Piero Bernardone well to the foreground, joined the clerical chorus. Presently fewer and fewer doors would be opened to admit the brown-smocked men. At Assisi and elsewhere they would be sometimes manhandled and accused of heresy, their services rejected as roughly as though they were lepers. But the poor all over the countryside never refused them. Among the unblessed folk affection and gratitude went on spreading.

A minor crisis came one spring morning when the men of the fellowship were at prayer in the tiny chapel of Rivo-Torto. A burly farmer pushed himself and his donkey into the house, and shouted that the place belonged to him as much as to them and that he meant to settle down there. Francis' temper flamed out in rebuke, but he did not stop to argue with the man.

There was no question of their going to Assisi or any other town. Surprisingly enough, the Abbot of Monte Subasio came to their aid. He let them have Portiuncula and some land in its neighborhood for

the peppercorn rent of an annual basketful of roaches.
The company sang their *Te Deum* with real joy. Soon
they built wooden huts round about the little chapel
and started to cultivate a vegetable plot in a clearing
of the forest. The monks were kindly. The basket
of fish would be acknowledged by a small jar of oil,
and from time to time a priest would come down
from the abbey and say Mass at Portiuncula.

Then Bishop Guido decided to gird his loins for
action. He felt that the cathedral chapter would give
him no peace unless he were to yield to their importunity, and he was anxious that Rome should not
hear any reports of his negligence in the matter. He
started by summoning Francis to the palace.

The message reached Francis at a difficult moment.

The move to Portiuncula had produced an unexpected reaction among some of the brothers. Here
and there were heard murmurs that prayer and contemplation were more rewarding than field labor,
domestic work, and care for lepers. Two or three men
began voicing their longing for life in a hermitage.
Francis heard these murmurs and they saddened him,
but he had nothing to say except that the dissenters
were free to leave Portiuncula at any time. Nobody
left and murmuring ceased, but Francis wondered if
the Bishop's wholly unexpected summons would not
create another difficulty for his fellowship.

Guido received him kindly and offered him a meal
which Francis refused saying he had done nothing
to earn it. Then the Bishop commended all the good
works done at Portiuncula, and Francis said that all
such praise should be given to God Whom they tried

to serve. These words provided Guido with an opening he had not hoped for. He blandly suggested that
Francis and all the others should join the Camaldoli
or any other recognized community. Francis replied
that monasticism was not for him and that he knew
his own call had come to him from Jesus. Guido at
once accused him of pride, and Francis kept silent.

All in all, it could not be called a profitable inter-
view for either host or guest, and it ended in a stalemate because the two men were talking of matters
neither understood. Francis knew himself called to
share with the whole world the joy given him. The
Bishop was convinced that no religious vocations
could be realized under the conditions of Portiuncula.
He said that there should be a properly drawn-up
Rule confirmed by ecclesiastical authorities. To a
Bishop of the thirteenth century the very idea that a
Rule could be given by no other than Jesus suggested
a blending of blasphemy and heresy. Guido refrained
from threats and sent Francis away, saying that he
would like to see him again.

Bishop Guido certainly had something of a case—
however clumsily he handled it both then and later.

Francis' ideal was blindingly clear to himself, but
he never made the least allowance for his contemporaries' inability to see it. Nor did he understand
that a great many things done by him and his company ran sharply counter to the generally accepted
standards. A religious profession, argued the critics,
meant first and foremost a total renunciation of the
world, and how could such a renunciation be compatible with an ardent passion for nature? Francis'
answer that Jesus loved flowers was no answer to

them. Again, a total renunciation implied a hatred of
the flesh because of the Fall. Francis called his body
"brother ass," but he could not hate it because he
regarded it as God's handiwork, and to him all hatred
of the flesh was sin because at the Incarnation God's
Son chose to put it on. There, again, was his love
of all created things. Untutored in any theological
subtleties, he accepted the Creed in its literal sense.
"Maker of all things, visible and invisible . . . by
Whom all things were made," from the body of man
to the leaf of a celandine, from a feathery cloud to
the most delicate rill in the valley. Not to love nature
seemed to Francis an absolute negation of God's
power and generosity. God himself delighted in the
world He made, and was it not ungrateful of man
not to share in the delight? Christ said that the lilies
in the field were far richer than King Solomon's
raiment.

Francis explained it all, but he did not understand
that such a point of view was wholly novel to his
generation, and he did not see why they should be
suspicious of it.

In his turn, the Bishop of Assisi was left with
his perplexity unsolved. Here was a young layman
known to him, Guido, since childhood, who admitted
that there was no salvation outside the Church and
was faithful to her ordinances, and yet was capable
of flouting her authority by preaching when he had
no right to do so, and by rejecting all suggestions that
he should test his vocation within some recognized
monastic pattern.

Back at Portiuncula, Francis gave much thought
to the problem. The very idea of an organization

seemed repellent to him, but in the end he came to admit that it was his duty to win papal recognition for his fellowship. He did not wish to ask for any protection from clerical attacks but he hoped that some such action on the part of the Roman Curia would confirm his liberty of serving God according to what he believed was the will of Jesus.

For all his lack of experience, Francis knew that it would be futile to go to Rome with nothing except his words to prove his case. So, helped by some of the brothers, he started working on a Rule wholly based on evangelical precepts. It was a short and simple document. Among others, it contained one telling clause: "Whoever should come to the brothers, be he friend or enemy, thief or robber, let him be kindly received," yet another departure from contemporary custom.

In the summer of 1210, Francis, accompanied by eleven brothers, left Portiuncula for Rome. Before the departure, he suggested that one among them should be to the others as the Vicar of Christ along the journey. "Wherever it may please him to go we will go, and when he may wish to stop anywhere to sleep there we will stop." Brother Bernardo was chosen by them all as the leader of the little expedition.

Francis had been to Rome as a pilgrim. Now he was going on business, but he carried no letters of recommendation, and he knew no one of importance at the papal court. None of it troubled either him or his companions. They went "singing and full of joy."

Innocent III had been elected Pope in 1198, as successor to Celestine III, the latter little more than a broken reed of a pontiff. In one sense, Innocent might be regarded as a successor to Gregory VII. A genius of an administrator, a zealot in defending ecclesiastical privileges, showing no mercy to prelates and clergy convicted of simony and concubinage, tireless in suppressing heresy, Innocent III was certainly a great Pope, and the weight of papal power come to be greatly increased during his reign. From Aragon to England, kings paid him homage. He sent legates to Scandinavia and encouraged Sweden to convert the heathen Finns. He was energetic in promoting the crusading movement, and any missionary was certain of winning his favor.

But Innocent III hated evil immeasurably more than he loved good. Jealous for the temporal dignities of the Church, guarding her lands against the imperial aggression, and her teaching from the heretical taint, statesman, judge, and general, he remained a man with a locked iron casket for a heart. He invites a comparison with Knox and Calvin. It is easy to understand why his death meant "joy rather than grief" to Christendom, to quote a thirteenth-century source (". . . *laetitiam potius quam tristitiam generavit subjectis*. . . ."). There was nothing for him to fear from the son of an Umbrian mercer. Conversely, Francis' horizons swept far larger ranges than Innocent III could ever see.

The little band had no easy time in Rome. The compassion of a few men and women of good will ensured them what few daily necessities they needed, but those benefactors had no means of introducing Francis to the Pope. Oddly enough, it was Guido of Assisi who unwittingly paved the way to the gates of the Lateran. Guido had come to Rome on some

business of his own. Happening to hear of the arrival
of "the brown-clad beggars," he lost no time in
acquainting Cardinal Ugolino, then Bishop of Ostia,
with "the beggars' case." Guido had never expected
Ugolino to show much interest in the matter. All the
Assisian wished was to safeguard himself from any
possible future awkwardness.

But the Cardinal was more intelligent than Guido
and he saw that such enthusiasm, once guided into
proper channels, would be of immense advantage to
the Church. Guido told him that Francis' following
grew most alarmingly and that many priests in
Umbria looked upon him as a heretic. But to a theologian of Ugolino's standing, the opinion of country
clergy meant little more than a wisp of hay.

"I must see the man," he told Guido. "Should he
be a heretic, it would be easy enough to silence him
forever."

So they met, the Pope's nephew, an aristocrat,
second to none, Innocent excepted, in ecclesiastical
eminence, and a barefooted little man in a shabby
brown frock whose credentials were a matter for
mockery among so many Umbrian clergy. But, looking at him, Ugolino wondered if Francis could indeed
be a mercer's son—his manners were those of a prince.

Yet the courtesy immediately approved by the
Cardinal was not the heart of the matter. He liked
Francis, but personal reaction could not interfere
with the judgment to be passed on his work.

So there followed many tedious sessions in the
Cardinal's palace. In the end Ugolino found himself
unable to see a single trace of heresy in Francis.
Flaming enthusiasm, sincerity, and rare single-

mindedness, all were there. "We can use him,"
thought Ugolino, "and I must present him to my
uncle." And to Francis he said: "I understand that
you wish the Holy Father to approve your Rule." The
little man replied courteously but firmly that he had
no such wish: he had come to Rome seeking recognition and not approval.

"The Rule came to me from Jesus Himself," he
explained.

Ugolino made no comment on such a bold claim.
Instead, he started his persuasions. There were many
religious houses throughout the length and breadth of
Italy which would welcome Francis and his men.
The Cardinal spoke eloquently about the need for
new breaths in monastic foundations. The piety,
fervor, and sincerity of the Umbrians could do much
good and certainly succeed in lending strength to
any enfeebled foundation.

Francis heard him to the end, then said there was
not a single religious house for them to enter. "The
least important priory, my lord, is cumbered with
possessions, yes, in this country and elsewhere—as I
understand. Now the very tunics we wear do not
belong to us. Portiuncula is not ours, and I do not
wish my brothers ever to own a square inch of land.
Jesus is my master and I serve Him and the Lady
Poverty."

Such words, if spoken by anyone else, would have
been arrogant and even rude, but Francis' manner
lent them a quality which more than ever convinced
his host of the little man's humility. The Cardinal
no more understood Francis' ideals than anyone else,
yet the experienced statesman could not but seize the

opportunity here presented. "These are very dangerous days for the Church," thought Ugolino. "This
little man might prove useful as soon as we have
persuaded him to discard some of his extraordinary
ideas. Surely, his humility will prove a great help."

That momentous meeting of Francis and Cardinal
Ugolino in Rome in 1210 marked the beginning of
a close and lifelong friendship between the two men,
a link all the more remarkable since neither understood the other's purposes. The Cardinal, from the
first attracted by the little man's honesty, gentleness,
and enthusiasm, at once saw in him an instrument to
advance the cause of the Church Militant, such service, however, to be determined by the directions from
the hierarchy. Francis, conscious of Ugolino's genuine
good will, came to regard him as a friend and counselor. At the beginning, at least, neither of the men
suspected that they were using a language alien to
each in turn. Francis' rocklike loyalty to the Church
did not exclude his firm belief that the life led by him
and his companions had been commanded by the
Lord Himself, and was to be accepted by the Church.
To the Cardinal, the mere idea of a dedication to the
Lady Poverty seemed little more than a dream. The
relationship between the two men would lead to
rather surprising ramifications. Here let it be said
that each man had a case.

Ugolino was experienced enough to see that, left
wholly to himself, Francis would achieve little more
than sporadic bursts of enthusiasm among his hearers.
Administration and organization were not found in
Francis' vocabulary. To Ugolino, then, belongs the
honor of establishing a religious order which, how-

ever distant from the Founder's ideal, would prove of inestimable value to the Church. Francis' claim to immortality rests on a wholly different basis. His life would remain a proof—never to grow dusty or stale—that man cannot live by bread alone.

In the end, the Cardinal took the little Rule and promised Francis that it would be shown to the Pope. More waiting followed. Francis felt no anxiety. He spent most of his time in prayer in one church or another. Presently he was summoned to the Lateran, and he went as he was—his hair unkempt, his bare feet dusty and scarred. He knelt at the foot of the Pope's throne and heard that the Rule by him submitted was beyond anyone's strength since, in Innocent's opinion, nobody could live "without any possessions."

Francis' reply, "Holy Father, Our Lord had not a pillow for His head," might have moved a Leo the Great. It did not move Innocent III, who belonged so wholly to his age that to his mind an attempt to return to Gospel simplicities was no more and no less than a fantasy born in a dreamer's heart. He did not reply. He merely repeated the suggestion earlier made by Ugolino that Francis and his men should prove their vocational fitness under the roof of a cloister.

Innocent had heard from his nephew about the little Umbrian's humility, and Francis' instant reaction to the suggestion rather took the Pope aback. Francis was humble indeed but in a way which had nothing to say to mere servility, and he answered boldly that he knew God had not called him to be a monk. Innocent remarked that such singularity could well have been born of spiritual pride, and Francis was dismissed, his purpose unachieved.

The brothers all but lost heart.

Bishop Guido had many friends in Rome, and he had neither wasted his time nor spared his eloquence in blackening the repute of "the brown-clad beggars." Ugolino stood alone in his promises of friendship and support. All the prelates assembled in Rome recoiled from what they labeled "a new and dangerous heresy." Some among them had been present during the audience given to Francis, and they alleged that his demeanor in the Pope's presence had been that of a braggart and an unmannerly fool. Francis was said to have interrupted the Pope and to have stamped his foot on leaving the hall. Absolute poverty indeed? Was he then going to live on air or else expect to receive manna from heaven? "Who could go through life possessing nothing at all?" stormed the prelates. "Does this insignificant little man from Umbria consider himself above all those who out of their piety had enriched the Church in the past? It is all very well for the Bishop of Ostia to say that the man is not a heretic. . . ." The prelates, urged on by venom and jealousy, were by no means certain that Ugolino was right. They dared not say so to his face, but they argued among themselves that—for all anyone knew —the Umbrian's loyalty to the Church was but a mask assumed for no other purpose than that of gaining his own perfidious ends. They hoped that someone might be courageous enough to suggest to the Pope that Francis should be dealt with in as severe a manner as had been shown in Lucius III's treatment of the Waldenses.

Some of the angry tittle tattle reached the brothers. They grew afraid and begged Francis to leave Rome instantly, but he refused to admit defeat even though Cardinal Ugolino happened to be away from the city for a little while.

"If we leave now," Francis told the brothers, "any Bishop in Umbria would say that we were condemned by the Holy Father. We might even be forbidden to nurse the lepers."

They all trusted him, but even his faithful Bernardo lost his cheerfulness. There seemed nothing they could do.

And then, unsummoned, and all but turned away from the gates of the Lateran, Francis succeeded in seeing Innocent III for the second time and told him a parable about a beautiful beggar woman married to a great king. When her sons were born, she decided to withdraw to the desert where she had been born, but when her sons grew to manhood, she sent them back to the King's court, and he received them with great joy.

"Holy Father," added Francis, "I am that beggar woman, and the Lord has not despised the sons I have brought Him."

The stubbornness, the simplicity, and the sincerity ended by moving Innocent III. He told Francis that, subject to episcopal approval, he and his companions would be free to preach. The Pope added that he thought it essential for the fellowship to have a man at the head, and he named Francis for the office. "You will come and see us again later on," concluded the Pope, and dismissed Francis with a blessing. Not a word more had been said about the Rule.

Francis accepted it all for true minted coin. He had liked Ugolino from the first, and now he felt he could trust the Cardinal implicitly. He knew nothing about casuistry. Words spoken by anyone meant what they said. He did not know that every utterance of his had been most carefully weighed on clerical balances. It was enough for him that a Cardinal had brought him to the Lateran and that the Vicar of Christ had given him his blessing. He had not betrayed his vocation by asking for a single privilege. He had come asking for recognition and not for protection. Anchored to an unimpeachable orthodoxy as he was, Francis considered his mission richly fulfilled and he was overjoyed.

And so were his eleven brothers. They went back to Umbria, and all along the way, so later the book *The Three Companions* would tell us, ". . . they found kindly souls who sheltered them, and they felt beyond a doubt that God was taking care of them."

In chilly reality, that very vague recognition accorded to Francis would mark the beginning of the end of the Franciscan dawn. Neither the Cardinal nor the Pope ever understood Francis' ideal. They chose to see him as a man who could fight all the ills then cancering the Church, and they were tranquilly determined not to let him use any other weapons save those fashioned by tradition. That Francis' calling was pre-eminently a creative one, that he was able to fight all manner of iniquity by a love scarcely understood in his generation, that in his eyes the matter of absolute poverty was a happy necessity rather than a terrible hardihood, all those were not even accidentals to the Pope and Ugolino. His faith

they were now sure of. The contagion of his fervor
they did not deny. All else was immaterial.

Given the world's conditions at the time, it could
not have happened any other way. That brilliant singularity, shining like a constellation over the darkened
and troubled Christendom, could not really have endured for a single generation. It was a revolt on a
well-nigh cosmic scale against the shameful dwarfing
of the Gospel—but it was a revolt which expressed
itself in peace, and the world met it with an un-
sheathed sword. To be loyal to the Church and at the
same time to remind her about things she should
never have forgotten was a Herculean task, and Francis was no Hercules. Nonetheless, that Franciscan
dawn, even though about to vanish off the Christian
sky, would leave much of its fragrance to all the
generations to come.

CHAPTER FIVE

THE MORNING

FRANCIS joined his companions in their laughter and singing all through the return journey to Umbria; he was truly happy, although the Cardinal's persuasions had left a sediment in the mind.

To Francis, the Will of God and the will of the Church stood together, no cleavage between them in any spiritual matter. But now it seemed as though the particular calling he had accepted as God's Will for him and his companions ran counter to the purposes of the Church. He had no doubts about the first. He had no certainty about the second, and at this point it should be necessary to emphasize Francis' remarkable genius in bringing together the irreconcilables. The Vicar of Christ and the prelates urged him to enter an established order. The Lord he followed wished him to continue in the way of absolute poverty. Neither then nor later did Francis allow his true vocation to lessen his loyalty to the Church.

Francis never knew that on his return to Rome, the Cardinal went to the Pope to have a lengthy discussion about the Umbrian matter. Ugolino had studied mankind as well as theology. It was clear to him that in Francis he had met a man with something like a morning star for a soul, a man, moreover, possessed by a passion to share his joy with his own kind and not to spare himself in his efforts to bring them nearer to the light seen by him. But the Cardinal

also guessed that Francis was not a man to steer his
rapidly growing fellowship through the endless demands, frets, and complications shaped by the conditions of the day. Portiuncula, as Ugolino saw, was but
a mustard seed—to be nursed with great care and pa-
tience. Its growth, let alone its maturity, would entail
labors far beyond Francis' abilities. He had confessed
himself dedicated to the service of the Lady Poverty.
Such terms of service excluded the rudiments of
administration, and Ugolino sensed that the very word
would carry no meaning to Francis solely because it
had never been used in Galilee.

The little man knew none of this, and the sediment
in his mind was still very faint, and often vanished
altogether. The return to the valley and the tumultuous welcome accorded by the tattered rank and file
of the city greatly heartened him and his brothers.
True, the clergy were still watching jealously, but
not even Bishop Guido dared oppose papal wishes,
and the freedom of the cathedral and other churches
was now offered to "the beggar" in his shabby brown
tunic, his appearance most uninviting, and nothing
but his voice possessing a magic which could turn a
November midnight into an April dawn.

Of course Francis' voice alone could never have
drawn the crowds. It was chiefly, as the author thinks,
his deep intimacy with God which served for a mag-
net. To use a somewhat crude comparison, God's love
was a sea and Francis' hours of prayer were so many
pitchers he would draw up—not for his soul's comfort only but for sharing with anyone in need. If
his touch healed the infirmities of the body, his mere
presence turned despair into hope for many, and

eased ills no physician could have cured. His words were not always honey. He would not evade the grim consequences of evil committed, and the Devil and his works were as real to Francis as they were to every man and woman of his day. But the keynote of every sermon was a love which fulfilled itself by loving and was immeasurably stronger than sin.

Now, crowds from all over Umbria and even beyond rushed to hear him, and Francis did not confine his preaching to church interiors. He went into the square and the streets of the city. He shared his joy, hope, and gratitude with people met far outside the walls of Assisi, in fields and along river banks, at farm gates, and on the outskirts of forests.

People came to listen because they felt he meant them to share the riches that were his. He never shaped his words according to his audience: noble and peasant, wealthy and poor, they were all alike his brothers and God's children. For the dry crust of didactic moralizing, he offered living immediacies. Man's happiness, he would tell them, stemmed from a true turning Godwards, and such a turning implied a genuine refusal of sin. All ill-gotten gains must be given up, all enmities healed, all uncharitable thoughts checked at birth, and all of it was to be done in the name of Love Incarnate.

There was nothing new in any of it, but the ancient truths gleamed like stars because he was able to speak them with a peculiar clarity and a deep conviction of one who had held communion with his Lord and theirs.

"You have heard it said that you should give alms to the poor so that your reward may be great in heaven, but the blessedness lies in the poor man's acceptance of your gift. Charity looks for no other reward." Many such sayings would later be recorded in *The Mirror of Perfection*. "Our life in this world should be such that anyone seeing how we live, would be drawn to praise God. You and I preach of peace— we must have it possess our hearts. . . ."

At least some of those seeds fell on the soil hungry to receive them. Assisi, in sad accord with many other Italian communes, was just then at the threshold of yet another civil war, its working folk clamoring for better pay, easier taxes, and the bestowal of civic privilege denied to them by the authorities. The have-nots certainly had their case, but they could not be said to improve it since violence was the only weapon in their armory. Nobility, clergy, and merchants, all of them anxious and hesitant, opposed the demands of the "rabble," even though some among them argued that they should be prepared to make concessions if only to save their goods and chattels from looting.

The situation tautened. But day by day, in sunshine and in blinding rain, Francis would march into Assisi and take his stand either in the square or at a street corner, and there preach on peace until both haves and have-nots came to see the futility of trying to resolve an apparent impasse by violent means.

So on a November day in 1210, a formal agreement was signed in the town hall, binding the *majores* and the *minores*, men of substance and the poor of Assisi, "to promise . . . with a common accord . . . to do all there may be to do for the honor, safety and advantage of the Commune of Assisi. . . ." The agree-

ment signed, all the haves and have-nots heard a
solemn Mass at San Rufino, followed by a *Te Deum*,
and it is permissible to think that none sang it as
joyfully as Francis.

The agreement led to the immediate abandonment
of many feudal rights, to easier taxes, and sterner
penalties for graft and extortion on the part of the
municipal officials. The red-stippled phantom of civil
strife faded from the Assisian scene for many years
to come. When devotees began showering extravagant
praise on Francis, he at once rebuked them because
"the work of the Holy Spirit was never to be attributed to a sinner."

Majores and *minores* . . . the ancient distinction
having lost some of its bitterness, Francis decided to
call his fellowship *"Fratres Minores"*—i.e., "Little
Brothers," or "Brothers Minor," as they came to be
known all over Europe.

Yet there were some among the Assisian clergy
who looked upon it all with jaundiced eyes. They
could not forbid his preaching, but jealousy is never
slow to find outlets for its venom. They said to themselves that Rome was not round the corner and that
the Pope was too busy to give much more thought to
"the beggar." Cautiously and furtively they began
spreading calumnies in every corner of Umbria.
Francis Bernardone "posed" as Brother Superior of a
nonexistent order. The Pope having urged him to
enter an established cloister, he had refused to do so
because of his pride. Was he not something of a
magician known to worship trees, running water, and
birds? He insisted that his vocation had come from
Jesus Himself. Was that not another proof of arro-

gance? His outward demeanor seemed humble enough,
but he sought nobody's counsel in spiritual matters,
and was that in accordance with true humility?

The more bitterly the clergy attacked Francis, the
greater grew his respect for their office and his loyalty
to the Church. With the whole of Europe riddled by
fantastic heresies, he would keep his orthodoxy to
the end.

They spread many calumnies by word of mouth,
but they did not dare to interfere with his work—as
yet. And in the spring of 1211 Francis sent some of
his brothers on their first mission away from Umbria.

It was a bold step, and—from a practical point of
view—a most imprudent one, but the early Franciscan
splendors had no affinity with prudence.

Francis was sending his brothers "to the lost sheep
of the house of Israel," but they were his own dearly
loved sheep and he their dedicated shepherd. Yet he
was sending them out without a thought of the many
wolves they were likely to meet on their wanderings
far beyond the familiar Umbrian scene. The very
real danger of brigands apart, those first Franciscan
missionaries had nothing to protect them against the
possible episcopal anger and condemnation or against
the hostile reaction of secular authorities. They had
no other credentials to establish their identity than
the words taught them by Francis: "We are penitents,
natives of the city of Assisi," but such credentials
were about as useful as a sieve held under a tap, because the Brothers Minor in no way resembled traditional penitents. They carried no candles, they did
not wear sackcloth, they did not burst into loud tears
because of their sins. Their gaiety, their obvious

pleasure in what beauty they saw around them, and, finally, their singing, all of it together warred against the accustomed idea of penitence.

Nonetheless, Francis sent them out, and his parting instructions struck a novel note at a time when any devout Catholic was first and foremost concerned with the salvation of his own soul. "God in His goodness has called us not merely to save ourselves but also many others. Commit all your cares to Him, and He will care for you."

Two by two, the brothers left Portiuncula, making for the North. They went barefoot and bareheaded, neither scrip nor staff in their hands. Once they found themselves beyond the Umbrian border, their reception became rather streaky. It was kindly enough in villages where people listened to them and did not grudge what alms they could offer, but even in the countryside there were folk who thought the brothers slightly mad for their refusal to accept food unless they had earned it by services. They met a far harsher climate in towns, particularly in Florence, Pisa, and Bologna where they were taken for obvious vagabonds and potential thieves. That impression deepened all the more because most of the missionaries had had but little practice at preaching, and their efforts led the hearers to dismiss them for impostors. Hunger, mockery, blows, and threats of imprisonment fell to their lot, but the spring in the land and the spring in their hearts were at one. In Bologna they had hoped to spend the night in the porch of a church but a merchant passing by did not think they were ordinary beggars and reported them to the watch. The brothers were expelled from the city with ignominy. They wished God's peace to the men who drove them away with many a kick and oath, and hardly were they outside the gates when they broke into singing. Certainly, "*joculatores Domini*" did not belie the name given them by Francis.

That first mission, undertaken in the teeth of all worldly prudence, was not wholly fruitless. Here and there, men, having listened to those very artless sermons, would move away from the crowd and pelt the brothers with questions. Where did they live? How many were they? Had the Pope heard of them? Were they really dedicated to absolute poverty? What was asked of anyone wishing to join their company? "Give up everything you possess" was the reply to the last question. "To your community?" "Ah no, we possess nothing at all. To the poor."

Some shrugged and went away. But others followed the brown-clad men, and eventually came to Portiuncula, their very last possession given up. There is a legend about a beggar who wept because he was certain they would refuse him since he had nothing at all to give up—"unless I go naked," he said, a tattered tunic summing up all his possessions. "But you are already one of us," they told him.

Among those first Franciscans, Brother Leo alone may be said to have fully understood Francis' ideal, but all of them were tranced by the joy of finding themselves free from the imprisonment of things, even though they may well have had a different image of the Lady Poverty than the one cherished by Francis. All were surprised by God and by the liberty His love and care afforded them. All were as loyal to the Church as Francis, but there was no exaggerated

piety in them, nor were they saints in the current
sense. The particolored raiment of self still clung
to most of them. The big and handsome Brother
Masseo all but surpassed Francis by his courteous
manner so that hardly a door was ever slammed in
his face, and the food he would bring back to
Portiuncula was always superior to the broken meats
received by other brethren. Masseo was given to occasional boasting: "Just a cart mended and a couple of
pigsties cleaned out, and look what I had for my
reward!" Also he had a streak of envy in him. "You
are not handsome," he once said to Francis, "you are
not nobly born, you have no great parts. Why is it
that so many people follow you?" And Francis replied: "Possibly because God could find nobody as
unworthy as I."

There was Brother Egidio, one of the very first to
join Francis, a man of humble birth and no startling
accomplishments. But he was loved for his humility
and for his gift of making a small loaf and a few
pickled fishes go a long way. There was Brother
Pietro, once acquainted with the silken ease of a rich
canonry, who gave it all up with the rapidity of a
swift's flight. Bernard, one of the wealthiest men in
Assisi, would have liked to bring embroidered cover-
lets and caskets of wine to Rivo-Torto if Francis had
let him. One of the most lovable and most difficult
brothers was Rufino, a nobleman and kinsman to a
woman soon to mean so much to Francis. Whenever
Rufino began to preach, people burst out laughing,
so odd was his delivery, so poor his vocabulary.
Crowds terrified him and he longed for a hermit's life
in some cave in the Apennines. Yet in the end, he

was one of the Three Companions to write the most
moving and truthful account of Francis' life. Another
of the Companions was Brother Angelo, whose singing would have silenced a nightingale, and Elias, a
man of humble birth, exceptional gifts, and no small
ambition for the Fellowship, Elias of Cortona,
spiritual brother to Innocent III and Cardinal Ugolino
rather than to Francis.

There were also anomalies. With Brother Juniper
we seem to catch a breath of something like a Vic-
torian music hall. Thoughtless, generous, simple to
the point of apparent idiocy, causing endless embar-
rassments to the brethren, and yet loved by them all,
Juniper never succeeded in growing up. Once he
fooled about in the kitchen of Portiuncula, cooking
hens in their feathers and eggs in their shells together
in a big cauldron. He wept bitterly when the brothers
recoiled from the mess. But the incident of the pig's
foot throws a different and sharp light—not on Brother
Juniper, a child of an age which recked nothing of
physical cruelty, but on Francis, the same Francis
whose tenderness to all living things so bewildered
his contemporaries. He was known to avoid treading
on a worm or a beetle because to him all life carried
the signature of the Creator.

The story is well enough known. Here it is given
briefly.

A friar at Portiuncula had been gravely ill, and
Juniper nursing him all through. When convalescing,
the man expressed a wish to dine off a pig's trotter.
There was not a morsel of any meat in the house.
Juniper armed himself with a kitchen knife, made
off for the nearest wood and came on a herd of

peacefully rooting pigs. He seized one of them, cut off one of its feet, and hurried back to cook it, but the screams of the animal roused the swineherd. In the end, the pig's angry owner appeared at Portiuncula.

And what was Francis' reaction? Indifferent to the agony of the maimed animal, he poured his wrath over Juniper for taking a liberty with another man's property. Here, Francis seems to have stepped back into the past he disowned: he became an honest merchant's honest son. In some such fashion he would have rebuked anyone among his father's assistants discovered to have pilfered a neighboring shop.

The incident is unpleasant, but it carries its own value. Had Francis always kept to dizzy spiritual heights, his stature would have been dwarfed—always except in the eyes of purblind hagiographers, but the daily rub evidently produced its inevitable blisters. Though his habitual courtesy never gave way to rudeness, the gentleness could and did occasionally vanish in sternness and anger. In a strangely satisfying manner, Francis' lapses from sensibility, his undeniable blunders and absurdities succeed in weaving themselves into the quality of the whole, and the result carries great attraction.

From the writings of those who spent those first years with him, it is clear how deeply Francis had imbued them with his own love of nature.

A medieval layman had but a fragmentary knowledge of the Old Testament. We are unable to gauge the extent of Francis' acquaintance with it, always

apart from the Psalter which he knew by heart, but
the Book of Genesis certainly spoke to the poet in
him. He interpreted Creation in the only possible
terms acceptable to a poetic imagination—those of
the greatest love story known to the world. The six
days of the Bible were so many expressions of Love
delighting in its power to create. To Francis, "all
things made" were so many signs-manuals of that
Love. Those who companioned him closely would
later remember that ". . . we who were with him
used to see him rejoice within and without, as it were,
in all things created, so that touching or seeing them,
his spirit seemed to be not on earth but in heaven. . . ."

The last words need qualification. In certain moments Francis indeed seemed "to be not on earth"—
but on a bridge which linked the world visible to the
world invisible. The sense afforded by that landscape
had no vocabulary known to man; nothing could be
explained but all things could be accepted and used to
enlarge the horizon known to the flesh.

Born in one of the loveliest parts of Europe, Francis had loved his native country since his childhood.
After his conversion, the delight in nature became a
song of joy. In that world of wild, difficult but always
enchanting beauty, with rocky summits, waterfalls,
deep forests, inaccessible peaks, and smiling valleys,
he moved about, an intimate of its light and dark,
its savagery and kindliness. The smallest evidence of
life evoked an extraordinary response from him. At
a certain level, he and creation, both animate and in-
animate, spoke the same wordless language. To his
eyes, a woodbine and a rose, though disparate, were
equal in glory. He reverenced the very stones he trod.

He could share hours of praise or contemplation with
running water, with silver birches and tamarisks. At
times, we are tempted to imagine a very faint thread
of animism running through that part of the canvas.

But some of the stories clustered round about
Francis' passion for nature rather tend to belittle his
truth. For instance, the legend about a night spent by
him in singing God's praises alternately with a
nightingale suggests—and that in spite of its beauty
—one of many efforts to enhance his saintliness. That
Francis moved in music both heard and unheard, is
a self-evident truth which has no need to borrow any
colors from legend. "In the beginning was the Word"
and ". . . by Whom all things were made" formed a
perfect musical phrase in his soul. In nature he saw
an indifference wholly alien to man's callousness, an
anger, and a darkness worlds apart from man's wrath
and midnight. Anchored as he was in the Catholic
faith, he accepted all the evidences of the world's
wounds as so many consequences of the Fall and the
never-ceasing activities of the Devil. Man had been
meant to enjoy the world in song and laughter.
Thomas of Celano, Francis' honest biographer, would
later remember that ". . . at times I have seen him
draw a stick across his arm, in the manner of one
drawing a viol, and [hear him] sing in French the
praises of the Lord."

Larks were his favorite birds. Once he told his
friends that if he ever had an opportunity to approach
the Emperor, he would beg him to pass a law to
prohibit the killing of larks. ". . . also that men in
authority should be commanded to see to it that
everyone according to his substance was to leave

wheat outside the door on Christmas Day for the comfort of birds, and that in memory of the Holy Night, all oxen and asses should have the best of good fodder upon that day. . . . For the Lord's love, all should provide largely not only for the poor, but also for animals and birds. . . ."

For Francis the only barrier between man and the rest of creation was fear—unworthy of man and insulting to the Creator. He held that fear in man engendered fear in the animals he met and that the animal's fear found an outlet in ferocity. Nowhere is this idea of Francis' illustrated as clearly as in the story about the savage wolf of Gubbio. Once stripped of all pious and fantastic detail, the incident images a singular victory over terror. The beast had become such a menace to the people of Gubbio that at the end ". . . it came to such a pass that . . . no man dared go outside the city walls for fear of being killed. . . ." When Francis heard about it, he "put his trust in God." He went out alone, none having the courage to follow him except at a cautious distance. Presently, the brute appeared, and some of the people far behind Francis closed their eyes in anguish—so certain were they that they would never see him come back. The little man made the sign of the Cross and spoke, calling the beast "brother wolf" and rebuking him for all the wickednesses he had done. The wolf, though ready to pounce, became very quiet, and then lay at Francis' feet. "He lived in the city for two years . . . and [he] was fed by the people . . . [and] never a dog barked at him, and the citizens grieved . . . at his death from old age."

The story has often been discredited—largely, one

would think, because of the many embroideries woven into the central episode, such as the wolf's solemn promise of repentance. But its core does not seem to belong to legendary lore. It accords well with Francis' truth.

CHAPTER SIX

THE LADY POVERTY
ENFLESHED

VERY firmly did the early Fathers of the Church pin
the colors of virginity to the ecclesiastical mast. In
canon after canon, in sermon after sermon, in prose,
and in verse, they extolled virginity as the flower of
all the virtues. Marriage was a sacrament, but the
ascetic point of view looked upon it as a sanctified con-
cession to the frailty of human nature. Widows and
widowers were urged not to remarry but to consecrate
the remnants of their lives to the service of the Lord.

Such arguments, passionately propounded by theologians and fortified by many apposite scriptural quotations, were oddly wanting in logic because of the
unequivocal command to the human race that they
should increase and multiply, and the patristic esti-
mate of womankind was out of all accord with the
veneration paid to the mother of the Lord. The arid
influence of that unbridled hatred of sex, having
reached its peak at the birth of the Middle Ages,
began declining a little, although the ideal of virginity, however illogical, never lost its pride of place.

All the canonical ordinances notwithstanding,
sexual morality was no worse and no better under the
Christian dispensation than it had been in the pagan
past. For the medieval laity, sex did not lurk in dark
corners. For one thing, everyday conditions did not
lend themselves to much reticence, if any. Even in

the lord's castle, curtains did not always screen the lord's bed, and further down the social ladder, the consummation of marriage would often be witnessed by relatives and friends. Both copulation and childbirth were primarily regarded as natural processes. Yet many ways of nature, being beyond the medieval comprehension, had to be propitiated. Thus, both marriage and labor were surrounded by a mesh of superstitious precautions, all of them borrowed from pagan ancestors and obeyed far more stringently than were clerical directions. The Church ordained continence at vigils and during fasts, and imposed harsh penances for the defilement of the marriage bed, but such penances were usually graded in accordance with the sinner's social status. The same classification was followed in cases of sexual aberration. A common man, convicted of sodomy, would be burned alive. His social superior would have to go on a pilgrimage to atone for the same offense.

In broad terms, the lay approach to sex was direct, shorn of all sentimentality, and decidedly brutal on the male side. At the top rung of the social ladder boys and girls were given in marriage by contract, their parents' choice governed by dynastical, political, and —pre-eminently so—physical reasons. To breed healthy children and to breed in quick succession was the wife's most important business. If a bride showed no signs of pregnancy within the first six months of marriage, she would be regarded with suspicion by her in-laws. If she was to fail altogether, she ran the risk of being unwifed and of spending the rest of her life in a nunnery. A childless marriage was all too often regarded as a sign of God's displeasure with a particular union, and on such grounds the Church sometimes permitted an annulment.

On the lower social levels, matrimony seldom if ever went beyond purely physical frontiers. Peasants' sons would be given mates whose health warranted their capacity not only to breed but to share to the utmost in all the tasks falling to the peasants' lot. That condition did not change after the birth of the age of chivalry in the eleventh century—in spite of a very palpable contradiction. Hardly a village in Christendom but possessed its shrine to the Madonna. The honor paid to Christ's mother came as naturally as breathing, but the mothers of men were all too often regarded as stud mares.

The age of chivalry, into which Francis was born, changed the climate among the higher social ranks. The new order of knighthood asked for delicacy and immediacy in the homage paid to the feminine principle. Romantic love came in with the passion-laden songs of troubadours, with debates on the theme of love at courts and in castles. Any knight, once his service was accepted by a lady, vowed not to spare himself on her behalf. During tournaments, a fleeting glance from her, a flutter of her veil, let alone her smile, heightened his resolve not to be unseated in the combat. Her glove given to the victor was an even more precious possession than his knight's spurs.

Thus, a once remote ideal received an embodiment. It was but natural—though by no means so in every case—for such worship to end in a mutual surrender to the physical urge. Yet even when thus resolved, the romantic element would not yield pride of place to the contractual. Marriage remained an indispensable social condition, sanctified by the Church. Romantic love, whether translated into physical terms or not, walked in its own rose-embowered garden where lawfully wedded couples would hardly have felt at ease.

Francis' youth had not been spent either at court or in a castle, but his acquaintance with the romantic climate had begun early enough. His enthusiasm for the troubadours' songs had soon led him to emulate their passionate mood in verses of his own. A little later, his friends had introduced him into a circle where by birth he did not belong, and the secret lettering of many a scene witnessed on the tournament field had become clear enough for him.

It is indeed strange that not a single feminine name had ever been coupled with his—even during his wildest spells. Of his charm, of his gift to captivate, we know enough. Assisi, on a par with all other Italian cities of the day, did not lack prostitutes. But Francis' most venemous enemies, charging him with dishonesty, pride, heresy, and witchcraft, could never accuse him of a single lapse, let alone continual debauchery.

Then came his conversion, and he fell in love with an ideal. A virgin neophyte, he swore devotion and loyalty to the Lady Poverty.

At a later date, the ideal became concretized and enfleshed, and love possessed Francis much in the same way as scent possesses a rose's petals. It was a love which made no demands and fulfilled itself in loving. He had served his Lady Poverty from afar. Now her embodiment was found to walk the same earth as was trodden by his own feet.

In a spiritual sense, Francis and Clare were truly and insolubly espoused, and theirs was a union of

which even an ideal earthly marriage was but a pale
reflection. They shared the holiest known to man.
They understood and trusted each other to the utmost.
Their mutual fulfillment and delight needed no
bridges to sustain them. Often and often, they held
communion when apart from each other. Each to each
was child, brother and sister, counselor, consort and
spouse. Francis never had to explain himself to her.
It might almost be said that unspoken words served
to unite them more closely. They moved together, one
ideal guiding them, within a liberty which all but beggared language.

Twelve years younger than Francis, Clare came
from an old, noble, and warlike stock, the Sciffi. They
owned much land in Umbria and had a fortified
mansion at Assisi. From what little we know, the
Countess brought up her two daughters, Clare and
Agnes, in such a manner that the girls were early
taught to spend much time in prayer, to care for the
poor, and to think less of themselves than of others.
The mother's influence, however, could not always
combat the father's wishes. His position in the city
and the neighborhood would make it inevitable for
his daughters to take part in many festivities. Clare
and Agnes were beautiful, and their father's wealth
permitted the purchase of exquisite clothes and fine
jewels. But Clare at least was known and loved away
from castles and manors: the poor of Assisi early
learned that her care of them went further than
prayers and words of compassion.

The Sciffi were a clan more than a family, and
neither the Count nor his numerous male relations
wished to see either of the girls enter religion.

It can be assumed that Clare heard about "the

brown-clad beggars" of Rivo-Torto and Portiuncula
early enough. That she was far from satisfied with
the life she was leading is obvious from the decision
taken by her. Her character was a blending of extreme gentleness and an almost rocklike firmness. All
she heard about Portiuncula stirred her to the very
depths. It seemed an answer to so many questions
she had asked of herself. Was it enough to sell a
jewel now and again to ease the hard lot of the poor?
Was it enough to fast, to spend a few appointed hours
at prayer, to go to Mass and Vespers at the Cathedral,
to be sorry for her sins, to approach God's altar with
as deep a devotion as she knew herself capable of?
Was there not something else, something of a wholeness she could not as yet see, that was being asked of
her? A life spent entirely for God and that not just
for the purpose of saving her own soul but for the
sake of many. It was all novel, rather shattering, and
almost beyond her strength. In view of later events, it
seems permissible to suppose that Clare's mother who,
on her husband's death, would become Sister Ortolana
at San Damiano, knew about her daughter's spiritual
travail.

Both legend and piety have clothed the story with
the abruptness of a miracle. In reality, Clare must
have heard Francis preach before that momentous
Palm Sunday in 1212. There is no record of any
earlier meetings, but a few at least must have taken
place—with her mother's full knowledge—and by that
time Clare knew what was being asked of her. God
and the Lady Poverty could surely be served by
women as well as men. So they had private speech
together, that young, determined, fervent girl of six-

teen, in her velvet cloak and silken gown, jewels at
her throat, and embroidered shoes on her delicate
small feet, and the man of mean appearance and
short stature in the frayed brown tunic of an Umbrian
shepherd, his feet bare, dusty, and scarred. When
Francis heard Clare speak, he learned her truth, and
that was enough.

On Palm Sunday in 1212, Clare and Agnes went
to Mass at San Rufino. Later in the day, Francis
preached in the square, and Clare heard him. She
stood in the crowd, but she was alone. She had faced
a challenge and made her reply to it. Now, all seemed
silence within her, but it was a strangely eloquent
silence speaking in accents which captivated, comforted, and awed Clare in turn. She had walked in a
wilderness grown thick with weeds. She was about
to enter a field rich with the promise of a fair harvest.

The people of Assisi were very dear to her. She
had known all its stones since her childhood. Now,
as she left the square to enter her father's house, she
knew she would never again be seen in those winding
narrow streets, but her resolve did not waver. Francis
was expecting her. Before that Palm Sunday came to
its close, Clare, companioned by her two trusted
friends, left her father's house for good. "By stealth,"
says the biographer, but it is obvious that her mother
and sister knew all about it. The three girls made
their way to Portiuncula where "the little beggar"
and his companions were waiting for them, lit torches
in their hands and the *Te Deum* on their lips. Under
some trees close to the chapel, the friars had spread
a coarse brown tunic and a hempen girdle. Helped
by her friends, Clare changed her silks and velvets

for the garb of the poorest among the poor, took off the gold-embroidered shoes and all the jewelry she was wearing, and, her two friends following her, made her way into the tiny chapel.

What followed was a marvelous inconsistency on Francis' part. He was not a priest. He never tired of preaching loyalty and obedience to the Church, but that night he made dust of episcopal authority and prerogative. In the tiny candlelit chapel he received Clare's vows, cut off her hair, and put a veil on her head. Then, accompanied by a few friars, he brought her to the Benedictine priory at Bastia in the neighborhood.

The very next day a tumult broke out at Count Sciffi's castle. The father swore to reclaim the daughter "stolen away by the beggars." Some friends having obligingly told him she was at Bastia, the Count ordered a few armed attendants to follow him and all but stormed his way into the priory. But Clare stood firm, and her father rather surprisingly was reluctant to use force.

He rode back to Assisi, vowing not to spare any efforts in bringing Portiuncula down to the dust. But the Prioress of Bastia was frightened and sent a message to Francis. She would not be able to keep the young lady longer than a few days, said the Prioress. It was her duty not to jeopardize the safety of her house. The Count would be certain to carry his complaint to the Bishop. The Prioress of Bastia was a woman of deep prudence.

Francis installed Clare in another temporary refuge at a house where the superior would not permit herself to be afraid of possible consequences, but it was not a house where Clare could follow the Franciscan Rule, and the arrangement had to be regarded as a makeshift. The crisis was sharpened when Agnes and a number of other girls from Assisi decided to follow in Clare's steps. In the end, the monks of Monte Subasio once again came to the rescue. They told Francis that Clare and all the others could have San Damiano in perpetuity. Some friars from Portiuncula went at once to prepare the place by building a few more huts and by clearing a plot for a garden. Presently, the little sisterhood settled there among the olive trees. They lived under the Rule followed at Portiuncula. Prayer and meditation apart, those first Poor Clares spent their time in working in the garden, spinning and weaving for the friars, and we know that Francis would send "many sick persons to San Damiano whom [the sisters] restored to health by the sign of the Holy Cross and by their prayers," to quote from *The Little Flowers*.

Whatever the Founder's inconsistencies, the friars' apostolate was not for the sisters. But to Clare the vow of poverty was absolute. They depended on what food was brought to their gate, and on lean days they went without. Nothing but the scantiest provision for the sick sisters was kept at San Damiano. The sisters, some of whom came from as rich houses as Clare's, slept on thin layers of straw spread on the ground, with a stone or a block of wood for a pillow, and they conformed to the observance of Portiuncula in all other particulars. A single trestle and a roughly timbered table summed up the furniture. What food they had would be spread on the ground.

But Clare was no grim recluse. She took as much

delight in birds, animals, and flowers as Francis did. She and her sisters would sing at work, so "possessed by joy" were they. A friar from Portiuncula, who was a priest, ministered to them, and warm currents of affection, understanding, and encouragement ran between the two places even though Clare and the others did not leave San Damiano. Whenever Francis was in the neighborhood, he visited her and "gave her holy instruction."

The Sciffi family brought their complaint to Bishop Guido who, however, shook all responsibility from his shoulders by suggesting that the count should take the matter to Rome. But Innocent III, counseled by Cardinal Ugolino, refused to interfere beyond advising Clare and the others to accept the Benedictine Rule. She would not do so either then or later.

Everybody in the neighborhood knew that the Sciffi girls would have brought enormous dowries to their bridegrooms. All they had brought with them was at once given to the poor, and with Clare's coming Francis' ideal of the Lady Poverty became enfleshed to the end of his days. Her superior, counselor, and friend, he was also her child. Her courage and steadfastness were there to offer him comfort; as the years went on, Francis would need her strength, serenity, and courage more and more.

Now the dedicated knight was at Portiuncula, the lady by him chosen remained at San Damiano, and the tournament became a combat of love against hatred, of peace against war.

Such a comparison need not be taken as an extravagance, because the knight never died in Francis. The apostolate in Umbria and beyond was but a beginning. Little by little he grew convinced that God required his presence away from Italy, and his hunger to see the Holy Land deepened. He would often discuss it with Clare. She, having met a number of crusaders at her father's castle, urged him to start on a crusade of peace.

Ever since the capture of Jerusalem by the Seljukian Turks in 1071, the matter of the Holy Places had been gripping the attention of Christendom. Not until 1095, however, did the Emperor of Byzantium succeed in persuading Pope Urban II to call a crusade. In 1099, with Jerusalem once again in Christian hands, Christendom felt that all those sanctuaries would be kept secure in perpetuity, but lack of cohesion among the Franks, their constant jealousies and quarrels, soon began playing into the infidel hands and shaping one reverse after another.

The fall of Jerusalem in 1187 plunged Christendom into mourning and also stirred a shamed consciousness of having failed their Lord. Once again fervor burned high and fresh efforts were made, but by the end of the Fourth Crusade in 1204, the last bulwark against Islam was more or less shattered because of a greatly enfeebled Byzantium. The Turks were entrenched in Palestine. At the Sultan's pleasure, a certain number of pilgrims were permitted to visit the Holy Places, a humiliation not easily accepted by the knighthood of Europe.

The Holy Land became the reproachful symbol of an unfulfilled Epiphany. With the True Cross in infidel hands, the Garden of Gethsemane trodden by infidel feet, and indifferent alien eyes looking upon Calvary, there seemed little enough for Christian comfort. The names of Nazareth, Capernaum, Bethany, and the Sea of Galilee were spoken longingly by those who had once crossed over to Palestine and whose hope of seeing those places again was growing fainter every year.

Between 1213 and 1215 Francis made two attempts to reach the Holy Land. The first venture carried him no farther than the coast of Dalmatia. His ship was wrecked, he could not find another to take him eastward, and he crossed the Adriatic again to get home. The second attempt brought him and his companions to Spain where the numerous hardships of the long journey told on Francis' none too robust physique, and he fell ill.

He recovered, but his condition did not allow him to continue the journey, and by slow stages he came back to Umbria. At San Damiano, Clare, steadfastly following in the steps of the Lady Poverty, kept assuring him that he would not die without seeing the Holy Land, and Francis believed her.

By then the Poor Clares had so increased in number that new foundations had to be made. One such was at Monticelli near Florence where Clare's sister, Agnes, went as superior. Clare herself was in her early twenties. Having never traveled beyond Umbria, she was intelligent enough to encompass more than the map of Europe in her mind. Every fresh missionary venture from Portiuncula was followed by her with keen interest. She never wavered in her conviction that Francis' ideals were necessary for the world. She encouraged, counseled, and chided him in turn. In a sense, he was both delight and anguish to her. But first and foremost he remained—after the Lord—her glory. His frequent visits to San Damiano were golden occasions—except in one detail. Clare was mistress there, and it grieved her that Francis would never dine with the sisters, nor indeed accept any refreshment. She urged him on several occasions and he always refused. At last, a friar who had accompanied Francis to San Damiano said to him, "Such a small thing she asks of you—and why don't you consent? All of us think you should. It would comfort her so much to have you break bread with her even but once."

Francis gave in but decided that Clare should come to Portiuncula for dinner. "It will be good for her to see the friary." He chose the day and sent a friar to San Damiano with a brief message for Clare and another sister to come to Portiuncula on a certain day. The other ladies were horrified. They took the message to mean that Francis intended their Clare to leave San Damiano and to start another foundation elsewhere, and many sisters wept when Clare and her companion left for Portiuncula.

There, Brother Leo told them that they were invited to dinner; he and a few other friars took the ladies all over the place, and Clare lingered in the little chapel where her dedication had taken place.

Meanwhile Francis was busy in the tiny kitchen, getting together what poor provender the house had that day. At last, so the biographer tells us, "he made ready the table on the bare ground as he was wont to do. And for the first dish he discoursed on God sweetly, loftily, and wondrously." His two guests and all the friars present were "rapt." Then he stopped and remembered his duties of a host, but neither Clare nor her companion took much heed of bodily food.

So the eyewitnesses say, and we cannot tell if the

two ladies left Portiuncula with their physical hunger unsatisfied, though Clare's good breeding would certainly have warred against refusing "the broken meats." We know that they left Portiuncula much comforted, and on their return to San Damiano were greeted by shouts of joy from all the others.

That was the only occasion when Clare left San Damiano during her many years in religion.

She was never robust and the hardships of the life soon enough came to tell on her physique. We do not know the nature of her ailments—but there is a wealth of detail about her fortitude, cheerfulness, and pleasure in the flowers and trees of San Damiano. The book of *The Little Flowers* is rather lavish with legends, some among them hard to accept, but at least one disarms all harshly critical approach by its simplicity and loveliness. It tells us about Clare's "grievous illness" one Christmastide. She had not the strength to leave her pallet and follow her sisters into the tiny chapel for the Office and the first Mass of Christmas. "But Christ, her Spouse, not wishing to leave her thus disconsolate, caused her to be borne miraculously to Portiuncula"—there to take part in the friars' Office and to make her communion. That done, Clare was borne back to San Damiano. Her sisters, their Mass over, came to tell her how deeply grieved they were not to have had her with them. Then, Clare, "wishing to turn their grief into joy," told them what the good Lord had done for her, and so they were all able "to share her rapture."

Such is the legend, and, within the context of Clare's life, it seems—paradoxically enough—clothed with reality remote from that of the senses. The experience, which does not lend itself to explanations, was real enough for Clare.

In common with Francis, she showed great humility and reverence in all her dealings with the hierarchy. Also in common with him she would defy even a Pope when the matter concerned the least deviation from the Franciscan Rule.

CHAPTER SEVEN

THE FIRST SHADOWS

AS the missionary journeys grew in frequency, not all the men wishing to follow Francis would be admitted by him into fellowship. Strictly speaking, those friars who went about preaching were not engaged in recruiting, yet hardly a day passed but someone, moved by the sincerity of their message and by their unfailing cheerfulness, would ask to join their company. Of such applicants nothing was required except a total renunciation of their possessions and the acceptance of the Rule. In such a fashion their numbers swelled so rapidly that by 1212 Portiuncula could not have contained even a tenth of the fellowship. Clusters of huts built of branches and reeds on what land was lent by local generosity appeared here and there, and quite a few of such centers were at a distance from Umbria.

In 1212, Francis decided to gather the entire company together at two annual chapters to be held at Whitsun and Michaelmas at Portiuncula which, although legally belonging to the Abbey of Monte Subasio, had come to be regarded as the Franciscan cradle. The great wood and the field sloping down into the valley were theirs by virtue of a lien far more enduring than any contract written on parchment. Together with San Damiano, Portiuncula was something of a rock, a light, and a warmth to them all.

The destinies of the two places were closely interwoven; there was a daily exchange of news, an exchange evoked by no shallow curiosity but by the mutual need of intercessory prayer. Not a single missionary journey would be planned at Portiuncula but its details were known at San Damiano and its success prayed for. From the material point of view, the friars were taught by Francis that the sisters' welfare was their concern. Seeds, plants, and roots for the vegetable garden, bread, fish, and oil, what fuel was required for the little kitchen, the only fireplace at San Damiano, all those came from Portiuncula. In return, the sisters did the friars' washing, "spun and wove" for them, made the hempen girdles, did all the mending, and sent what medicaments they made from the herbs they grew. When visitors came to San Damiano, the gifts they left would be shared with the friars down to the last egg. But prayer and counsel stood well to the forefront of all those exchanges.

The first Franciscan chapters were very much family occasions. Of sheer necessity, they would be held in the open air. No arrangements of any kind were made for the victualling. The people of the neighborhood saw to it that the friars lacked nothing. Mass and customary religious exercises apart, the friars gathered together in the field, reported the results of their missions, and all of them together mapped out the journeys for the future. That business over, they listened to Francis. He did not preach to them. He talked, as friend to friends. His words were always simple, but his hearers drew strength and refreshment from them. Again and again he would tell them never to lose their respect for priestly office in spite of all they might suffer at the hands of the hierarchy. He would impress on them the necessity for tolerance toward the hardhearted rich and of compassion rather than pity for the suffering of man and beast. But above all stood his words on God's love and God's peace. By that love they were surrounded and within it they worked. And once Francis said, "Brothers, you go and you preach about peace and you wish peace to both friend and enemy. Let it then wholly possess your hearts."

Each chapter over, Francis would bless them and send them away with an encouraging farewell. The *joculatores Domini* went singing on their way, both faith and hope reaffirmed once again. They were at one, God's care encompassed them, and they were rich because they possessed nothing at all.

But a wholly different mood crept into the Whitsun Chapter of 1215, and it left Francis plunged into the bitter waters of melancholy. His failure to reach Syria and Morocco and his long illness in Spain had been hard enough to bear. Now the first ripples of dissension among the fellowship still further darkened Francis' sky.

He did not understand that, the great numbers considered, some such dissensions were more or less inevitable. Moreover, his missionaries enjoyed the liberty of admitting new members, and not all the friars sent out from Portiuncula were infallible judges of character. All too often they took enflamed imagination for sober conviction and high-burning ardor for an unbreakable resolve to follow the Lady Poverty. Those who had joined the movement, after having seen Francis and listened to him, would forget that they were incapable of lighting the same flame in the hearts

of others. It was enough for them to realize that they
had delivered the message taught by him and that, as
they believed, the seed had fallen on fruitful ground.
They looked no further than that.

Few of the men admitted away from Portiuncula
fell away altogether, but quite a number of them
began to murmur against this and that detail in the
Rule. They had not understood that they were not to
accept even a stale loaf of bread unless they had done
some work to earn it. There were many little things
to chill the hearts of men more or less unprepared for
the Franciscan reality. The unabating clerical hostility smote them like a flail. They argued that the
hierarchy would be certain to alter their attitude if
the Brothers Minor were armed with a privilege from
the Roman Curia. No wonder, they murmured, that
they were considered as vagabonds when they had
no real settlements anywhere, and must depend on
casual generosity, and that all too often in those parts
of the country where they were not well known and
where people were suspicious of them.

All these plaints and many more were gathered up
together at the Whitsun Chapter of 1215. The malcontents spoke boldly enough, and the point most
labored was that they must win some privilege from
the Pope. At once, and indignantly, Francis repelled
the suggestion. That, in his eyes, was tantamount to
a broken trust in God's care.

There was yet another reason for the slowly growing discontent. To a large extent, the responsibility
for it must be laid at Francis' door.

His friars had preached in Bologna and Padua, and
a number of learned men had been admitted into the

company. In bald terms, they should never have been.
The leaven they had brought was good and rich, but
it did not belong to the Franciscan spirit.

More will be said later on about Francis' attitude
to learning. Here it is enough to state that the academic world, its demands, achievements, and splendors, meant nothing to him. Acquainted with the
Gospels and liturgies, ceaselessly learning the world
of nature, Francis asked for no more either for himself or his disciples. But it did not suffice for so many
who now wore the shepherd's brown tunic, and Francis could not see that imperceptibly his ideal was being
superseded by an idea. Friars like Elias of Cortona,
and prelates like Ugolino could see it clearly enough,
and the Cardinal certainly had good cause to be
pleased. But Francis noticed nothing except the
visible signs of discontent, and he was bewildered that
such sullenness of look and manner should have
found its way into the fellowship.

The chapter ended with the customary *Te Deum*,
but there was no joy in his heart.

Was he right to continue? Was the work by him
begun at all necessary? Had he misread God's will
for him? Should he abandon it, hide himself in some
remote hermitage, and spend his time in prayer and
solitude? These questions shattered his peace. Doubts
and hesitations cobwebbed his mind. He stayed on at
Portiuncula, his few intimates in despair. Not even
Brother Leo, Francis' "little sheep," could persuade
him to take some food. His health, weakened by the
long illness, worsened. Day by day, night by night,
Francis stayed motionless outside his cell, his soul like
a wanderer in a vast desert never visited by sunlight
or starlight, unfamiliar to the angels of God.

It was Clare who rescued him.

Worn out by the clawing uncertainty, Francis did not go to San Damiano, but he sent a trusted friend with a message, asking Clare to seek God's answer to his question—should he abandon it all and turn to a hermit's life?

The report brought by the friar about Francis' physical condition did not greatly surprise Clare. She knew that the long-drawn-out fever caught in Spain had greatly undermined his health. She knew about the sleepless nights, the pains in his head and legs, and the spells of exhaustion. But this time she sent no cordials to sustain him. Instead, she took, as it were, his melancholy into her hands and used it in the only way she knew: she offered it to God. There were occasions when her courage was greater than Francis', and this was one of them.

Together with the other sisters, she gave herself up to prayer. Her answer to Francis was unequivocal: God had not called him for himself alone but for the needs of the world. All those doubts came from the Evil One and they would be dispersed.

And dispersed they were the moment her reply reached Francis. With an athlete's agility he leaped out of the wilderness. Peace and tranquility possessed him again. He sang praises of the Lord, asked for a meal and ate it with appetite, and the same day, with Masseo and Angelo for companions, set out on an unplanned mission to the southwest of Assisi. Crossing a field near Bevagna, a small hamlet along the way, he heard some birds singing over his head. Francis halted, spoke to the birds, blessed them, and laughed for joy as he watched them vanish towards the blue cup of the sky. In that birdsong he heard, as it were, an end to his own anguished silence. Once again he himself became a song. Thomas of Celano would later record a deeply cherished memory: ". . . he loved to fly away like a bird and make his nest upon the mountains. . . ."

That summer mission of 1215 carried a sense of wings. Francis was indeed like a bird joyfully tranquil in the liberty afforded by the flight. The sermon to the birds at Bevagna was at once a covenant and an identification. Most clearly did it show Francis as emperor of his desire to be at one with the world made by the God he served. Yet the experience did not quite belong to his century, and few understood it. Later, the moving and lovely record would suffer much from the intrusion of garish sentimentality utterly alien to its truth.

By that time, himself all unconscious of it, Francis had become a source of light and a legend in Umbria and even beyond. The mocking cry "*Il pazzo! Il pazzo!*" had all but vanished from peoples' memories. If remembered at all, it brought burning shame into the heart. Francis' simplicity, his kindness, and, above all, the sense of his nearness to the Lord he served, all these unlocked many hidden rooms and swept the dust out of darkest, most neglected corners. However inarticulate were the common folk, they grasped that Francis considered them as men and women, and clothed them with an identity the rich and the mighty never permitted them to wear. To the latter, they were so many pairs of hands to labor and so many pairs of feet to hurry to do the bidding of their masters. To Francis, they were brothers and sisters, all of them together members of God's household. Their bitter lot stirred his compassion, which had nothing to say to shallow pity, still less sympathy. To the medieval man, "compassion" carried the meaning of its Latin root and meant a share in the other's suffering.

Compassionate as he was, Francis never urged the poor to rebel against their lot, not only because he saw that violence would end by increasing their misery but because, ceaselessly speaking about peace, he lived within its climate. His words released the best in many. San Fabiano, Narni, Rieti, Greccio, Gubbio, Fonte-Colombo, and many other places were now peopled by those enabled to breathe more amply because of his coming and going.

During that particular missionary journey in the summer of 1215, the beating of birds' wings seemed to continue all through. At Siena, in the crowded market square, Francis released several turtledoves from their cages, a bystander's instant generosity quelling the stallholder's anger. At Rieti, he was delighted to find that many robins had made themselves at home in the tiny friary. They flew in and out of the cells, the kitchen, and the small refectory, making frequent inroads into the meagre provender—to the indignation of the cook. "They ate all the cheese yesterday," he complained to Francis.

"Brother," replied the little man, "have you forgotten the words 'freely you have received; freely give'?"

All along the way, birds flocked at the first sound of Francis' voice, perched on his shoulders and hands, pecked at the hem of his tunic, and sang to him. On the shore of a little lake, seeing a number of ducks, he knelt at the water's lip and held converse with them. What country folk were around looked on,

awed and enchanted. A few monks passing by halted
and frowned. They might have shrugged and laughed
if the fowl were drakes, but ducks, being of the
feminine species, were to be kept at a distance. Francis' contemporaries in religion feared sex even more
than they feared the Devil. It was not enough to
prohibit women's entrance into the enclosure: hens,
duck, turkey hens, cows, she-asses, mares, and nanny
goats were likewise excluded. Essential for the monastic economy as they were, they would be kept outside—at a safe distance from the sacred grounds.

That joyous summer came to an end. In November
1215, the Fourth Lateran Council pronounced a
formal ban on the formation of religious foundations.
The rumor of such a measure had reached Francis
earlier in the autumn. He would often go to San
Damiano, ask for the sisters' prayers, and discuss
the matter with Clare. So far the official attitude had
gone no farther than Cardinal Ugolino's persuasions
that both Portiuncula and San Damiano should adopt
the Benedictine Rule. But persuasions were not com-
mands.

Clare offered no advice. She prayed for a way to
be shown to them. Francis was not troubled on his
own account. He knew where he stood, but he could
not forget the Whitsun Chapter and all the voices
raised in dissent. So many of the brothers were away
on southern missions. He could not tell if some would
find their way to Rome and there win the Cardinal's
attention. At once the little man rebuked himself for
the unworthy thought. But it would never have en-
tered his mind the year before.

Clare had an answer to her prayers. Francis should

go to Rome, and he went, with about twenty friars.

Ugolino was glad of his coming for a very particular reason. There was another visitor in Rome and the Cardinal wished the two men to meet. Both were passionately sincere and enthusiastic. Both were unswerving in their loyalty to the Church. Ugolino's secret hope was to see those two men join their work together for the greater benefit of Christendom. But the Cardinal, shrewd judge of character though he was, failed in this instance. The road trodden by Dominic was not the one Francis could ever walk.

The two men met and liked each other exceedingly. They exchanged their missionary experiences, and Francis was keenly interested to hear that Dominic's men had been working in Paris and in various German cities. "And what about the German bishops?" he asked, and heard that so far Dominic's disciples had met with no opposition from the hierarchy.

There followed a very difficult session with Ugolino. The Council, sitting at the Lateran, had pronounced its ban, and the Cardinal immediately invited both Francis and Dominic to his palace. They must now choose some approved Rule for their foundations, he told them. Dominic did not hesitate. He said that he would like to accept the Augustinian Rule as a basis for his own. Francis sat buried in silence. When urged to give his answer, he replied that he was morally unable to abandon the Rule he had brought to the Pope in 1210. The Rule did not belong either to him or to any of his brethren: it was Christ's.

Ugolino had more or less expected such a reaction, and he had prepared most subtle arguments—all

based on fine theological premises familiar to Dominic
and utterly strange to Francis. He listened to them
all. He could refute none. He was neither theologian
nor rhetorician. He merely repeated that the Rule
he followed had been given to him by Jesus, and he
remained as firm as the rocks in his native country.
He was no rebel against the Church, but he dared
not compromise with the Gospels.

The Cardinal decided to try an easier and more
practical approach. He had heard, he said, that the
Brothers Minor often experienced difficulties when
trying to preach in towns where they were not well
known. The reason was clear enough: they had no
protection from the Papal Curia. Surely, argued
Ugolino, Francis' most excellent work would greatly
prosper if his missionaries traveled about, their safety
and liberty assured by a papal privilege.

But that very word cast a slur on the idea of absolute poverty, as Francis saw it. Later, he would em-
body his feelings in his Testament where he wrote
that he firmly commanded ". . . all the brethren,
wherever they are, should not beg for any privilege
from the Roman Curia." Now he answered that he
knew all about the difficulties so often experienced
by the Brothers Minor, but they formed part of their
apostolate.

And the matter was left there.

But a real sorrow awaited him on his return to
Portiuncula. The friars who had accompanied him
to Rome told the brothers—sharp envy in their voices
—about all the privileges showered on the Dominicans
by the Pope. "No Bishop dare oppose them anywhere,
and here are we—having no protection at all. . . ."

That was a far heavier burden to bear than the
hostility of the hierarchy. It became still further ag-
gravated by the attitude of those scholars from
Bologna and elsewhere who were now members of the
community. With many a learned argument they
urged that most of their difficulties would be solved
once they went about with some papal document in
their armory. All the missionaries had carried them
in the past—even Columbanus did not scorn to receive
one from the King of the Franks.

It had been hard enough to listen to such talk in
Ugolino's palace. Here, at Portiuncula, it seemed un-
bearable. Rather sharply Francis reminded them that
in their eagerness to obtain a piece of perishable
parchment for their safety, they had forgotten that
they were surrounded by God's care on their right
hand and on their left.

"I desire this privilege from the Lord, that never
may I have any privilege from man. . . . If hostile
prelates choose to silence us for a time, let them do
so. The world can be converted by example as well as
by spoken word."

Francis did not really reproach the dissenters. He
did not speak in anger. But his obstinacy was rock-
hewn. He told Clare that the matter passed his comprehension: the Lord had given them riches beyond
dispute and yet they were longing for the miserly
alms of man. The Lord had given them the liberty
of His light and yet they were anxious to run into a
dark corner. Was that his fault, and where had he
failed them?

There was no failure, Clare told him. It was a
testing time, she thought, and the Devil was using

his most subtle wiles to disturb the foundation.
Francis believed her, but a mental climate he could
not understand ended by affecting his health for a
long time. Innocent III died in the summer of 1216.
His successor, Honorius III, began evoking the spirit
of crusades. Preparations were afoot all over Europe.
Early in 1217 several missions began getting ready
to leave for Syria. Francis had hoped to lead one from
Portiuncula, but his physical condition made it impossible.

The skies soon darkened further. Francis had not
yet met Honorius but he understood from Ugolino
that Innocent's successor was in sympathy with the
Franciscans. That was true enough, but Honorius
III understood Francis' ideals even less than Innocent
had done. The rumbles of the struggle to come grew
less and less distant.

And just about that time Francis stumbled into his
first major blunder, which became a trump card in
his enemies' hands.

He had not forgotten about the successes of
Dominic's missionaries in the German states. The
Brothers Minor had never broached that frontier.
Now, decided Francis, it was the right moment to
start his own missions in those countries. Accordingly,
numbers of friars were sent to Germany, to Hungary,
and to Spain. In Rome, Ugolino heard about it and
kept his own counsel.

The Franciscans knew neither the language nor
customs of those countries. The great physical hardships of such journeys apart, their reception was shattering. In particular, the German bishops, untiring
in their benevolence towards the Dominicans, lost no

time in showing their hostility to the Brothers Minor.
They were hounded from place to place. They did
not always escape imprisonment. The rigors of the
climate proved disastrous to men who had nothing but
tunics to wear summer and winter. In most of the
cities they visited, bishops forbade their preaching
outright. In the few places where the permission was
given, they were forced to speak through an in-
terpreter—with pitiful results. They fared no better
in Hungary. Those who went to Spain found themselves accused of heresy, and they might not have
escaped prison—or worse—if the Queen of Portugal
had not offered them shelter in her own country.

The men were not saints. Such searing experiences,
stemming from a total unpreparedness for strange
conditions, led to ever-thickening discords among
themselves. They all but lost heart, and were unaware
that they had begun weaving a curtain some day to
fall upon the ideal Francis had taught them. Ugolino
could never claim credit for the battle eventually won.
Inner dissensions were the cause of it.

Nonetheless, it cannot be emphasized too often that
a breath of that ideal remained to be remembered by
many who would come after.

It is a truism to say that any society postulates
an organization, its activities administered by men
capable of such steermanship as the society's purposes
demand. But Francis was neither organizer nor administrator. He was convinced that none but God's
hand should be at the helm. He had heard a call and
answered it to the fullness of his genius. He left everything else to Providence, and he did so in the most
literal sense. Genius he certainly had. Into a world

ribbed by vice and misery, marred and scarred by virtually unceasing violence, clogged by possessiveness, he had brought his own vision, all the colors dissolved in the terrible and compelling purity of white. The world as a whole would sometimes admire and again mock and censure, but it could never understand. Nor was it ever clear to Francis why the world failed to see what he saw. Still less could he comprehend why they kept offering him a stagnant pool of ecclesiastical bureauracy in exchange for the free running water of the Gospel stream.

He had accepted Ugolino's friendship and he trusted the man despite the many evidences to the contrary. Francis need not be accused of blindness in this instance. A man of his caliber could never have suspected that the statesman in the Cardinal had long since elbowed out the Christian.

After the accession of Honorius III, Ugolino went very deeply into the Franciscan matter. He knew that the movement had enflamed crowds in Umbria, Tuscany, Emilia, the March of Ancona, and elsewhere. Freely admitting the value of fervor, the Cardinal had no great trust in its permanence. More than ever the Church stood in need of reforms, and he still hoped that the Franciscan missionaries might be used as instruments. Now he remembered his earlier plan to join Francis' sons with those of Dominic. "The hounds of the Lord" were higher than ever in the favor of the hierarchy. They never puzzled or angered bishops. Dominic, said the bishops, did not ask impossibilities from those who joined him. They settled down in proper houses. They did not go about in rags and earn their victuals by menial work. They preached and they taught. More important, they

were untiring in their fight against heresy and being
learned men, they had many good weapons in their
armory. In a word, "the hounds of the Lord" went
with the day's current, their work standing beyond all
estimation in the Church's battle for orthodoxy.

Now, surely, was the right moment for uniting
them with the humble men from Umbria. With that
purpose in mind, the Cardinal summoned Francis to
Rome to preach before Honorius III and also to meet
Dominic again.

The two men met in charity and perfect courtesy,
and once again Dominic was enchanted by Francis'
simplicity and humility. "You are truly my friend,"
he said to the Poverello, "and surely, you are running
along the same course as I am. Let us then stand
together. In such a case, not a voice will be raised
against us." Dominic spoke sincerely enough although,
no doubt, he had had his instructions from the
Cardinal, and his last words were odd: not a voice
had so far been raised against "the hounds of the
Lord." Innocent III had loved them. Honorius held
them in high favor, and not a bishop in Christendom
but welcomed their arrival in his diocese.

Francis thanked Dominic for his generosity. "But,
dear brother, I must stand where I have stood from
the beginning—in obedience to the Lord Christ and
in service to the Lady Poverty." Dominic, who had
already accepted the Augustinian Rule as a base of
his own, might have replied that poverty was one of
the three monastic vows, but he was far too charitable
to engage in an argument. Their meeting ended in a
kiss of peace, Francis having warmly invited Dominic
to come to the Whitsun Chapter at Portiuncula.

Cardinal Ugolino heard about the meeting, but

he looked upon it as a preliminary, and he still hoped
to see the two movements united. It heartened him
to hear of Francis' invitation to Dominic. In his turn,
the Cardinal promised to come and to sing the opening
Mass.

It proved a memorable chapter indeed. Chroniclers
tell us that fully five thousand of the Brothers Minor
were present. The number quoted may well have
been exaggerated, but it is a fact that by 1218 the
friars were a great multitude. They overcrowded the
field and wood. When Dominic arrived, he was
astonished to find that nobody had thought to provide
food for them. "Brother," he remarked to Francis,
"Whitsun being a great feast, there is surely no
occasion to fast." He had already been inside the
friary and seen the few dried fish, some eggs, onions,
apples, and a little bread. He had said to the brother
in charge, "There are vast crowds to feed. Do you
then expect a miracle to happen at Portiuncula?" and
the friar had smiled. There was nothing to prevent a
miracle from happening, he had said to Dominic.

There was Francis, apparently unconcerned. "An
occasion to fast?" he echoed. "My guests and my
brothers are not going to fast. I have left it to God.
He always provides."

Later in the day, Dominic, standing at the top of
the crowded field, watched a long procession of laden
carts appear from the road to Assisi. Were they
going to some market town in the valley, he wondered, and then saw them all halt. It was the city's
annual offering to her saintly son and his company.
Bread, fruit, wine, vegetables, meat, fish, and oil were
brought in such quantities that the friars were hard

put to it to find room for all the gifts. Dominic
supped off well-broiled fish and some excellent cheese,
and Francis urged him to have wine. "My own
brothers," admitted Dominic, "seldom fare so well.
Why, in Germany they had to get accustomed to
black bread and thin beer." Francis replied: "My
brothers do not mind when they have to put up with
short commons, and they do so often enough when
away from Umbria. But even nettles can be eaten
gratefully since they were made by God."

The Cardinal stayed with Bishop Guido at Assisi
and rode over early the next morning to sing Mass
as he had promised, Francis serving as deacon.
Thousands of voices soared skyward, far above the
peak of Monte Subasio. "*Emitte spiritum tuum, et
creabuntur: et renovabis faciem terrae. . . .*" and the
face of the earth could indeed be renewed within
Christ's triumph from the Nativity to Pentecost. Francis, joining with the rest, felt that all the frets,
abrasions, and misgivings had gone off his sky.

The Mass came to an end. They all dined in the
open air. Then the chapter began, and it proved to
Francis' intimate companions that the dawn lay behind them and that the burdens of the noontide were
heavy indeed.

Malcontents had not lost time in laying their griev-
ances before the Cardinal and found an ally in him.
Suddenly there was a diversion from the routine.
Ugolino had a canopied chair prepared for him. But
he did not sit down. He beckoned to Francis, and
together they walked towards some trees at the back
of the chapel. Many friars in the multitude held their
breath. The dissenters smiled expectantly.

The first thing the Cardinal had to say was to suggest that the scholars among the Brothers Minor should be enabled to continue their studies and also be given a share in the government. Francis made no comment. To him, the Brothers Minor were not divided into scholars and illiterates. They were all one family—bound by the same vow. Francis was unable to allow of any difference between Brother Rufino, who had studied theology, and Brother Juniper, who would not have known what people meant when they spoke of syllogisms.

That suggestion of the Cardinal's was but a preface. He had something to say about Pope Honorius' deep respect for tradition, about the great good done by the Benedictines and the Augustinians, about the astonishing progress made by the Dominicans. Francis had heard it all before. He did not interrupt. When at last Ugolino stopped, Francis bowed courteously.

"I shall make my answer to the brothers, my lord," he said and led the Cardinal to his canopied chair. Then the little man turned, faced the great assembly, and began in a loud voice:

"Dearest brothers, the Lord has called me into the ways of simplicity and humility, and He showed the way for myself and for anyone who wished to join me. So I beg you not to come and speak to me of St. Benedict's Rule, St. Augustine's, St. Bernard's, or any other—but only of the one which God has seen fit to make open to us, and He does not wish us to have any other."

Here Francis paused. He realized that the malcontents of his family must have tried to prove their case among the high-placed men in the hierarchy. When he spoke again, his voice was no longer mild but charged with anger, and the searing words were aimed at those who were trying to introduce an alien leaven into his family.

"It is by your learning that you will come to confusion. Whether you will or not, you shall taste regret and I am certain that God will punish you."

The outburst was painfully honest. What had the way of a schoolman to do with the way of poverty? Or the happy temper of the *joculatores Domini* with the inevitable jealousies and rivalries of the academic life? Yet Francis should have remembered that he had never barred learned men from entering his family.

At the Whitsun Chapter of 1218 the sad rift was there for all to see. It did not displease Ugolino who still hoped, fond though he was of Francis, that "common sense" would win the day in the end. It did not displease Elias of Cortona and many others of the same bent. But the hearts of those closest to Francis were nearly broken.

As for Francis himself, he had no hesitation in joining issue with those who were trying to force his calling into a traditional frame. He was determined not to surrender and to continue the struggle for an ideal than which nothing purer and holier had been evidenced by the world since the birth of Christianity. He had never imagined that the entire world would follow him, but he was convinced that he was right to struggle for that liberty which, as he believed, had been accorded to him by Christ and enjoyed by those who had joined him.

The contemporary background considered, such a

battle was doomed to be lost from the very first, and the cleft in the once-united family would never again be healed.

Undoubtedly, Francis had much on his side. But, unfortunately, all his integrity notwithstanding, he showed a lack of justice and charity. The intrigues were bound to wound and anger him, but he did not see that some of the responsibility lay at his own door. He had always mistrusted the schoolmen and considered that the Franciscan ideal and learning were incompatible, but he had never reflected on the probable peril of sending his missionaries to Paris, Bologna, Montpelier, Padua, and Salerno. In a sense, it was a contradiction in terms, and the contradiction sharpened with every fresh admission of a learned clerk. It seemed enough for Francis to see such men dispossessing themselves of the very shoes on their feet. He never realized that the rich furniture of their minds was a possession not to be rid of except at the cost of betraying one of God's choicest gifts to mankind—the sweep and reach of creative thought. Francis would have been horrified at the mere idea of silencing a lark or a nightingale since to him they praised God by their singing, but he did not see that to imprison an active, well-trained, and well-furnished mind was an immeasurably greater offense. He, capable of pouring out his very soul in passionate praises of the Creator, was too blind to see that his obduracy in this particular darkened the splendor of his own vision. He should have conformed even more closely to the Galilean example and permitted none but the common folk to enter his family.

Yet, odd as it may appear, that cloak of fallibility

now fallen upon his shoulders helped to increase his
stature beyond what the most vehement hagiographers
saw in him. It set his feet more firmly on the ground
common to saint and sinner alike. It spanned whatever gulf there might have been between him and the
multitude of spiritually average men and women.

He felt bitter against the malcontents, but his attack on the learned men of the fellowship was unjusti-
fied. To use a pedestrian comparison, those men might
be likened to scientists of today who, having attained
the greatest eminence in their field, find themselves
at sea when trying to fry bacon and eggs.

More and more shadows came to darken the Franciscan sky during 1218. Among the olives of San
Damiano, Clare would spend whole nights praying
that Francis' spirit and courage might not fail him.
He had once brought her into the house of his joy.
Now she claimed her right to share in his sorrow. He
did not complain, but he sang less and less often,
and he composed no more songs.

Friars, back in Italy after their painful missionary
efforts in Germany and Hungary, brought a leaden
sense of frustration to Portiuncula. The story of their
failure soon left Umbria for Rome, and afforded
another opportunity for Ugolino. In the end, it was
comparatively easy for him to persuade Francis that
further defeats in the missionary field could be
avoided. This once *il Poverello* uttered no protests
when told that the Pope alone had the authority to
assure the friars of the protection they needed. Francis, having heard the sad chronicle of persecutions at
the hands of the German bishops, knew he could no
longer rebel.

So it happened that Honorius came to sign a document, a duly attested and sealed copy of which would now be carried by the leader of every Franciscan expedition beyond the Alps. ". . . we pray you . . . to receive as good Catholics the friars of the above mentioned society . . . and to treat them with kindness for the honor of God and out of consideration to us. . . ." The document was valuable and must be protected against the hazards of the weather. It could not be carried in a friar's hand. The sheet of parchment necessitated a scrip, an apparently infinitesimal detail—but it drove yet another nail into Francis' ideal of absolute poverty.

It was a signal victory for Ugolino and the cause of great joy among the dissenters. The Cardinal spared no efforts to make Francis see what great results were certain to stem from the measure since no bishop in Christendom would venture to disregard a papal signature. The paper certainly was an assurance of further victories in the missionary field. But to Francis it meant the falling of a curtain, and once again, it was Clare, who herself sorely harassed by prelates, made him see that even a fallen curtain might be raised if God so wished.

He could not avoid disillusionment, but he remembered that bitterness and despair were against the Rule he so cherished. Once again he was conscious of refreshment. Joy and happiness were a friar's necessity. Had he not written that the brothers should never give way to sadness and clouded temper and that they were to continue their work, constantly "rejoicing in the Lord" ("*gaudentes in Domino*")? Out of joy rose the perfect liberty of true observance.

That perfect liberty was a confirmation and not a contradiction of the friars' obedience. Absolute poverty being a *sine qua non*, Francis reckoned but little of lesser canonical precepts. His friars were not marionettes pulled here and there at the end of a wire held in the superior's hands. Their obedience bound them to the Rule and not to a person. Where a Cistercian had to ask leave before he could substitute his daily stint of hoeing for digging, a Franciscan, working in the garden, would use his own judgment as to whether he had better dig or hoe. Equally, Francis would often lighten the burden of "Brother ass," as he called the body, by relaxing the prevalent severity of fasting and abstinence. If a brother, having worked for a farmer all day long, received pieces of broiled meat for his fee, Francis did not pause to remember if the day were Thursday or Friday. They ate the meat in common, and praised God for the farmer's generosity.

The common folk knew nothing about the cleft in the family. Crowds flocked to hear Francis preach, many asked his counsel and prayers, and just as many expected miracles. Now the power to heal all manner of infirmity given by Christ to His disciples certainly belonged to Francis, but he used it most charily. The recorded miracles are comparatively few. Thomas of Celano devotes no more than ten paragraphs to them. Not all the recorded miracles can be traced to Francis directly: some people would be healed by touching things which had been handled by him. We know from the record left by his intimates that Francis, so eloquent on many themes, kept a most rigid reticence about all the cures, nor would he have his friars mention them except as "the work of the Lord," his own part in the healing excluded.

Clare supported him by her prayers, courage, and counsel throughout all the difficulties of those years, but not even she could spare him the anguish and torment falling to the lot of so many among their contemporaries.

In general terms, evil to Francis was as real as it should be to Christians of every age. But Francis, although in so many aspects far ahead of his generation, was staunchly medieval in his concretization of evil.

The ancient battleground had not changed down the centuries but the manner of the combat had become much more subtle. In the very early days of Christianity, asceticism frequently carried to revolting extremes, hatred of the body, well-nigh pathological ideas on sex, contempt of all visible beauty, and long spells of solitude could not but lead to most excruciating experiences of demoniac power, and those were experiences, not illusions. Hermits and others did not imagine both mental and physical assaults of the Devil. The genuine bodily anguish they suffered was probably the least of their torments.

In a certain sense, Francis was their inheritor. The conception of evil most dramatically fostered by pictorial representation certainly fed his imagination just as it fed the imagination of his contemporaries. Hell was as real to him as Paradise, and he believed that no man born of woman but had to battle—at some time or other—with the members of the cloven hoof, company ceaselessly engaged in teasing, tempting, and tormenting a Christian soul. The Middle Ages excelled in making most graphic records of evil interference with the human kind. The imagery may well have been exaggerated but the reality remained, and the closer one's consciousness of Supreme Good, the more fervent one's endeavors to follow it, the more savage were the Devil's attacks.

In Francis' case, those grim encounters were not often in the foreground, and it is significant that Giotto did not include a single demon in his great fresco of the saint's life.

More will be said about the matter later. Here it is enough to emphasize that with Francis, evil would assume forms which both his senses and his inheritance could recognize. The attacks were mental and physical, and the latter were by no means imaginary. Yet Francis was far better armored than any of his predecessors in that he loved Nature and hated nothing, sin excepted. It was precisely the strength of his armor that provoked the attacks.

CHAPTER EIGHT

THE HOLY LAND

TWICE had Francis tried to reach Palestine, and the
second attempt had gravely undermined his health,
but the urge to see the Holy Places never died in him.

The Crusade, already proclaimed in 1215 by Innocent III, began taking shape under his successor.
The flaming enthusiasm of the eleventh century
could not again be invoked. Nonetheless, Honorius'
call stirred a great many people to shame that un-
christened hands should defile the country infinitely
dear to the most lukewarm Christian. Once again
weeping crowds took to listening to fiery sermons
mostly preached in the open air. By the beginning
of 1217, thousands had taken the Cross and numbers
of religious communities decided to send small missions of their own to give spiritual help to the
crusaders. When the news reached Portiuncula, Francis at once decided to place himself at the head of the
little band about to take ship for Accra. Yet attacks
of intermittent fever and the general state of his health
prevented him from leaving Italy in 1217.

But Clare had once told him that he would not
die without seeing the Holy Land, and the events of
1218 made Francis long for some such refreshment.
A marked improvement in his health played its part
in making him come to a decision which was greatly
encouraged by Clare. He would go, Francis told her,
together with a few of his intimates, and preach not

only to the crusaders but also to the Saracens. He never lost hope that the Hallowed Land would one day be restored to the liberty of true worship.

To take the decision was simple enough. The arrangements that must now be made before Francis could leave Italy were many, and all of them wearying. The fraternity having grown tremendously since 1215, he could no longer leave Portiuncula to God's care and then hurry towards the coast on the wings of an instantly made decision. He realized this clearly enough but all of it irked and troubled him. Not until the early summer of 1219 were the last preparations completed.

It was necessary to relegate his authority, and Francis chose two men whom he thought he could trust wholeheartedly. One was Matteo of Narni, and the other Gregory of Naples, nephew of Cardinal Ugolino. Both were appointed as vicars during Francis' absence. Portiuncula was committed to Matteo's care, and Gregory was to look after Franciscan affairs throughout the peninsula. On the very eve of departure, Francis, having spent a long time in prayer, had the two friars in his cell for a private conference, and he emphasized the importance of their standing firm against all the possible demands which might be made by the malcontents in the family. Both Matteo and Gregory solemnly promised to abide by the Rule, and Francis felt he was free to go, no anxiety fretting him.

Together with eleven friars, Francis took ship at Ancona for Accra, which was reached in the middle of July. The time at sea had not been spent in idleness, the friars paying by hard work for their passage.

They landed, full of hope and fervor, and made for Egypt.

The crusaders' camp, at the time, was outside the walls of Damietta which they were besieging.

What Francis found in that enormous camp all but shattered him. He had long accustomed himself to look upon knighthood as a body of men whose pure intention, high valor, and unspotted honor was their proud signature. He had believed that any man, once having taken the Cross, was dedicated to the holiest purpose of the day. But here, up and down the enormous plain, perfidy, self-interest, and vice were treading a brazenly obvious measure. Harlots from Sicilian ports, from Byzantium, Rhodes, and Cyprus were living and plying a busy trade in luxuriously appointed tents. Hawkers of relics were shouting their wares at every corner. Francis learned that some knights were known to pawn their armor to pay a prostitute's fee or to buy a cask of wine. There were many chapels, and the camp teemed with priests and monks, but gluttony, drunkenness, and debauchery were in appalling evidence. There were also gambling dens and a huge market where everything could be bought—at a price—from a lady's favors to a bag of candied figs.

It happened on a Sunday, and all the chapel bells were ringing for Mass, but it did not take long for Francis to realize that a large number of knights and their attendants were in no fit condition to go to worship; many were lying in drunken stupor outside their tents.

It was an appalling introduction. Francis' companions wrung their hands and wondered if they

should make their way back to the coast. They had
not imagined that crusading matters could ever have
sunk to the level of shoddy commerce and vice. Nor
had Francis, but he refused to despair. And, little
by little, his presence made itself felt in that camp
outside Damietta. His capacity for anger had never
degenerated into a habit. He could indeed storm
occasionally, but his inherent gentleness always won
in the end.

He preached up and down that vast camp, and
the words stirred many to shame. His fervor was
more flaming than ever, and a number of crusaders
asked to join the Brothers Minor, among whom were
Colin, an Englishman, Matthew, rector of La Sainte
Chapelle, and quite a few German knights, as Celano
tells us in his biography. Thus, whatever Francis'
personal reactions were to the conditions found among
the crusaders, his mission proved rewarding.

The chronicler Jacques de Vitry was able to write
to a friend in Lorraine: ". . . Brother Francis is so
lovable that he is revered by all. Having come to our
camp, he was not afraid to go . . . to our enemies. . . .
For days together [he] preached the Word of God to
the Saracens, but with no success. . . ." Nonetheless,
the Sultan received him kindly and dismissed him
with honor. Christ's teachings having been civilly rejected, Christ's messenger had been neither interrupted nor insulted.

Francis returned to the camp and continued working there until the fall of Damietta. The ghastly sack
of the city by the same men who professed their faith
in the love of God brought Francis to the end of that
road. "So much evil spread among the Franks was

seen by Brother Francis," commented de Vitry, "that
he left us."

At this point all the biographers are silent except
to tell us that in November 1219 Francis and his
companions left for the Holy Land. They reached
it, but we have no other details. Eight months later,
at some unnamed spot an urgent message from Italy
reached Francis. In the summer of 1220 he was back
at Portiuncula. By the autumn the final crisis broke
upon him.

Troubles at home had thickened almost immediately after Francis' departure. The two vicars he
had trusted failed him from the start. Matteo of
Narni, suddenly and rather incredibly cowed by the
attitude taken by the malcontents, had decided that
it would be better for the whole family if he, Francis'
vicar, were to swim with the current. That, so
Matteo thought, at least made for peace. Gregory of
Naples, greatly influenced by his uncle the Cardinal,
took Elias of Cortona into his confidence. Certain
radical changes in the Rule were inevitable, said
Elias, and Gregory remembered all he had heard
from his uncle. The dissenters decided, however, to
wait until the Michaelmas Chapter of 1219.

That chapter ended in a tumult. The loyal adherents of the Rule defended their ground inch by
inch, but the protestants shouted down all the objec-
tions. Assured of the support in high clerical circles,
they were determined not to waste the chance afforded
by Francis' absence from Europe. The vow of absolute poverty must be eased, the Rule must be brought
into conformity with the existing religious orders,

and "proper" cloistral observances must be introduced
into the horarium. Most of those so-called proper observances were concerned with trivialities not worth
a moment's breath, but the loyal supporters of Francis
were scandalized by the least change likely to be
brought in during his absence and without his authority. To that particular objection the malcontents
replied that there was no higher authority than that
of the Pope and that they were going to Rome to
obtain his sanction.

They did not add that they had already been
instructed by Elias of Cortona, and that the proposed
changes would not be confined to clothing and fasting. Nothing was said about their intention to approach Ugolino in order to win many papal privileges
for the Brothers Minor.

The true servants of the Lady Poverty were in
despair. They knew they would never get a hearing
at the Papal Curia. The most eloquent spokesman
among them could not hope to out-argue a man of
Cardinal Ugolino's perspicacity, and he was the only
only person in Rome able to procure a papal audience
for the friars. The peace of Portiuncula was shattered
during those days, and the angry climate came to its
peak when a visitor from Assisi brought a rumor
of Francis' death in Palestine.

But neither the news about the tumultuous chapter nor the rumor of Francis' death could break the
tranquility at San Damiano. Clare, saddened by dissensions, refused to weaken in her allegiance to Francis' standard. She would not give credence to the
rumor about his death. Herself sharply harassed by
unceasing attempts to force San Damiano into the

Benedictine framework, she would not lose hope. It proved her finest hour. The loyal friars at Portiuncula were sustained by her example.

The rumor about Francis had reached Umbria by a devious enough route, but that did not lessen the horror it produced at Portiuncula. The friars heard that a merchant on his homeward way from Aleppo to Venice had fallen in with the squire of a French knight. The young man had been sent back to Europe because of his health, and he told the merchant that a terrible disease was scourging the crusaders' camp outside Damietta and that some missionaries from Europe had fallen victim to it. The squire said there could be no recovery from the attack. In Venice the merchant told the story to a Dominican friar from Germany. In due course, the rumor reached Augsburg. In the end, the story lent an identity to the dead missionaries. They were now known to have come from a place in Umbria. Their leader, a man of small stature, was the first to die, and they buried him with high honors. In such a garb, the story traveled down to Assisi, having gathered a good many details on the way.

The party of innovators now felt that their hands were untied. The loyalists refused to lose heart. In a secret session held at night in the heart of a wood they decided to send one of their own number across the sea to discover the truth. That done, there seemed nothing else left to plan for. With heavy hearts they watched the delegates' departure for Rome.

It took the friar a very long time to find Francis, and what was the news he brought? The disgraceful Michaelmas Chapter, the disloyalty of the two vicars,

Ugolino's tireless efforts to merge the Dominicans and Franciscans into one congregation, the actual enforcement of the Benedictine Rule upon the Poor Clares in Florence, Lucca, and Siena, the innovations proposed by the swelling numbers of malcontents, and the idea that any property held in the name of the community need not be considered in terms of an individual possession. The friar did not waste his time in telling Francis about the trivial changes so fervently desired by the malcontents.

Francis' first thought was of Clare. Immediately he wrote to her and sent the friar back to Europe, charging him to deliver the letter into Clare's own hands at San Damiano. "I beg you all . . . to persevere always in the most holy life of poverty, and take good care never to depart from it at the advice of anyone. . . ."

Then, with the least delay possible, the twelve friars took ship for Italy.

On Francis' return, the first blow fell upon him at Bologna. He and his companions were making their way to the house of a certain benefactor who always gave them shelter in return for their care of his poultry and bees. On the way they met an acquaintance who told them they had no need to go so far and pointed to an elegantly colonnaded house at the corner of the square. "Why, this is now known as the House of the Friars," he said. "It belongs to them." Anger welling up in him, "the poor man of Assisi" ran across the square, walked into the house, and ordered all the friars to leave it immediately. They protested that the place belonged to Cardinal Ugolino and that they were lodged there out of charity. That was true, but Francis had little use for facts at that moment. Even compassion seemed to desert him—the sick among the men were included in the expulsion order.

That friary at Bologna brought a searing revelation to Francis. Could those be the men who had vowed to keep poverty, he asked himself. He heard a friar unknown to him by name shout from the top of the stairs, "Oh, I must have a few moments to gather up *my* books. . . ." Another was loudly asking if anyone had seen *his* inkhorn and a bunch of quills he had *bought* the other day. Yet a third was fussing about a mislaid flask of mint cordial. The shrill voice of a brother cook could be clearly heard from the kitchen: "This barrel of herrings is far too heavy for me to lift. . . . There is so much food in the larder. . . . Must I leave it all behind? Here are all the cheeses bought by Brother Paulo—no, I mean they were given to him. . . . Oh Madonna, will someone help me to shift the herrings?"

Francis shook off the dust of Bologna as hurriedly as he could. Those men were none of his. All of them wore the coarse brown tunic, and all wore it dishonorably. He and they were strangers to one another. Followed by his stricken companions, Francis made his way south, lead in his heart and a thick mist in his thoughts.

He sent nine of the friars ahead to Portiuncula. He and the two others stopped for a retreat in a mountain wood close to the borders of Umbria. Francis spent that time entirely alone. The two friars attended to his wants as much or as little as he allowed them to do. He was spent physically, but he

knew that he needed solitude more sharply than ever
before. He must listen to God's voice and find the
guidance enabling him to see a way clear through
the darkness.

In the end, Francis came to a hard decision. He
went to Orvieto, there to meet Cardinal Ugolino and
to ask him to take the fraternity under his official
protection. It was no easy request to make, but
Francis realized that he was no longer able to breast
the storm of dissensions. He blamed none but himself.

It was one of the wisest decisions made by Francis.
At this point, it should be made clear that Cardinal
Ugolino was no wolf in sheep's clothing as de-
picted in some biographies. True he did not understand Francis' ideals, but he revered the man and all
he stood for. Nor could Ugolino be accused of any
intrigues carried behind Francis' back. The Cardinal
openly urged *il Poverello* to join forces with Dominic
and with equal candor argued that the Rule should
be brought within some measure of conformity with
the day's conditions. The friendship between the two
men remained deep and genuine to the end.

Now, having heard of Francis' return, Ugolino
expected him, and received him kindly. The request
was granted—but at a price. A year's formal novitiate
was made obligatory and a new Rule must be drawn
up, Ugolino explaining that the document of 1210
no longer complied with the needs of the fraternity.
Presently, the bull of Pope Honorius III, *Cum se-
cundum*, formally marked the Franciscan entry into
a world, its breath so alien to *il Poverello* that Francis
knew that his days at the helm were ended. So worn
out and ill did he feel that the realization brought

something like a sense of release. But the ideal, mis-
understood by practically all his contemporaries,
would never die in him, and it would inspire many
throughout the generations to come.

That faint sense of release proved most unhappily
fugitive. Francis was too human not to feel the wound
on him inflicted, and that in so base a manner. He
heard all about the studiedly exaggerated welcome the
dissenters had received in Rome during his absence
abroad, the honeyed words spoken to them, and the
choice meats offered for their delectation. More than
once Francis wondered if those men could ever have
been true sons of his, and then immediately he would
rebuke himself for lack of charity.

His request granted, Francis hoped to leave Orvieto
for Portiuncula, but the Cardinal explained that there
remained much for them to discuss. So Francis had
to spend many anguished days at Orvieto. The hours
were crowded by trivial discussions which seemed to
serve no other purpose than that of clouding Francis'
mind. He disciplined himself to listen to everything
said to him, but he could not help wondering if any
of these feather-light matters had anything to do with
him and his calling.

Should the friars be shod? If so, in what manner?
What shape should their footwear be? Sandals, most
probably, with a single thong, or perhaps two thongs
would be better. Should the friars not be allowed to
carry scrips or satchels? The hempen cord might well
be replaced by a properly woven girdle. Should the
girdle's color be brown or white? If eggs and milk
were to be forbidden on Mondays, should cheese be
allowed and if so, in what quantity? Should the vicars

be addressed as "Brother" or "Father?" On what feasts
should talking be permitted in the frater?

And then, all imperceptibly, discussions began
veering away from the trivial and brushing against
perilous reaches.

What about casual hermitages? Were they not
proving inconvenient since the numbers of friars were
growing so rapidly? Would it not be more compatible
with the future work of the Order for the friars to
live in convents when not engaged in missionary
work? Did it or did it not violate the vow of poverty,
always bearing in mind that everything from a field
down to the most battered cauldron in the kitchen
belonged to the community together and not to an
individual brother? Should there be guest houses at-
tached to the convents, and small charges made for
bed and board as was the custom of most existing
religious houses? But would it not be better to leave
such matters to the discretion of the guest? To whom
should the brother-treasurer be responsible—to the
superior alone or to the whole house? Would the vow
of poverty be broken if a friar, teaching at some university, received monetary fees for his work? What
did St. Augustine say? Or St. Clement? Or St. Bernard? They must not forget Lanfranc's Constitutions,
and there were many useful things to be found in
the writings of St. Anselm.

All those matters, Francis was civilly assured,
would come under discussion during the Michaelmas
Chapter. Everything would then be put to the vote
and not a single decision taken except in a perfectly
legal way.

None of it meant anything to Francis. Bemused

and sick at heart, he felt rather like a man who, having spent a spring morning in a fragrant wood, with birds and running water for companions and God's free sky for a roof, finds himself all too suddenly pushed into an airless little room, no view from its mean latticed windows, and someone's voice asking again and again: "Will you have beans with bacon, or without? That is the question."

Over and above everything else, Francis was obsessed by a sense of failure. "I have to give it all up," he thought, "and I must have failed from the very beginning."

One star alone shone in his sky. Clare stood firm in her loyalty to the ideal he cherished. Neither frightening rumors nor the most adroitly persuasive arguments could move her from her allegiance to the Rule.

There was nothing for joy at Portiuncula during the Michaelmas Chapter of 1220. The dissenters, smugly assured of support in high places, were not afraid of presenting their case, and they carried the day. One of the earliest Franciscan precepts, "you shall carry nothing with you," was abandoned with scarcely an argument in its defense.

At the end, Francis rose from the ground to tell the assembly that guided by God and his own conscience, he had decided to lay down the burden of leadership, and he went on to name one Pietro di Catana, a nobleman and a scholar of note, as the General of the Order. "From this day on," *il Poverello* went on slowly and a little unsteadily, "I am dead to you all. This is where now you owe your obedience, and so do I," and leaving his place, Francis went to kneel at Pietro's feet. Then, turning abruptly, Francis raised both arms and said in a voice, its sadness shaming many of those who had opposed him:

"Lord, You know that I have neither the strength nor the ability to look after the brothers, and I confide them to another's care—since such is Your Will."

Having spoken, Francis turned away from the gathering and made toward his cell.

For a moment all was silence. Then loud cries, gasps, and sighs echoed from end to end across the great field, but Francis did not appear again, and the chapter ended with Pietro di Catana in the chair.

That winter Francis embarked on no missionary journeys. He remained at Portiuncula, and tried to work at the revision of the 1210 Rule whenever his condition permitted it. That did not happen often. Mental fatigue, spells of exhausting fever, headaches, digestive disorders, and a persistent dull pain behind his eyes, such were some of the results of the years spent with not a moment's care for his own comfort. Angelo, Rufino, Bernardo, and, in particular, Leo, watched over him. There was a frequent exchange of messages with San Damiano, where a warm cloak was being woven for Francis, and a sister, possessed of great knowledge about the virtues of various herbs, kept making cordials to be sent to Portiuncula.

There was work for Francis to do, and it did not take him long to realize that the 1210 Rule could never lend itself to revision. It was little more than a brief document based on his own reading of the Gospels. To add even a single paragraph would have been tantamount to an unwarranted liberty taken with evangelical texts.

The Rule of 1221 is not very easy to read. To begin
with, it is rather long. It carries the imprint of deep
mental suffering. Some of the passages suggest that
they must have been drafted and even put into their
final form at a time when Francis' thoughts were
chaotic. He can be seen wandering from point to
point, and the sense of cohesion is lacking. There
is certainly some beauty in many of the passages,
but, taken as a whole, the 1221 variant suggests a
necklace, the stones strung together without much
concern for the general effect.

Writing, as such, had never come easily to Francis.
The poems and songs he composed would either be
learned by heart, or copied down by some of the
brothers to his dictation. Now his condition put all
writing out of the question. So Francis dictated paragraph by paragraph, little thought of any continuity
in his mind. The result was a collection of messages
and precepts from a father to his children. Joy, sorrow, regret, a touch of anger, staunchly anchored
hope, and reiterated references to the vow of absolute poverty, all are blended together in those pages.
"Let us always keep a home within ourselves . . . for
the Lord God. . . . Let nothing *again* [italics mine]
hinder, separate, or retard us. . . ."

Francis' hands were no longer at the helm, and he
must have forgotten those wearisome sessions at
Orvieto. It may well be that the 1221 Rule was composed for those who still remained faithful to their
original calling, who looked with loathing at the mere
idea of possessions, and did not care whether their
feet were sandaled or not.

The work finished, Francis felt deeply dissatisfied

with it. But he had no strength left to do any
more.

As was to be expected, the mere accents of the
manuscript failed to win the approval of the Roman
Curia. They had looked for a properly drawn up religious Rule. They had hoped for clarity and legality.
Over and above its several obscurities, the document
did not contain even a hint of legality as understood
by the canonists. And how could it be otherwise
when the only law understood and followed by Francis was the law of charity? Love subscribed to no
juridical pattern, and was governed by reasons not
to be found in codices.

About two years later, the Brothers Minor had a
Rule given to them, and Francis would play no part
in the drafting of it. The Rule of 1223 was un-
equivocally contractual. God's invitation became a
command, and man's reply to it came out of sub-
mission. Law, not love, traced the pattern, and
obedience to it carried an individual reward of eternal
bliss. *Joculatores Domini*, who were to fire the world
by their "joy in the Lord," became so many members
of yet another Order, all its activities subjected to
the scrutiny of the hierarchy. The contemporary clerical mind never grasped that Francis did not condemn
property as such any more than Jesus did. In Francis'
eyes, only those who had the true vocation for it had
the right and the duty to free themselves of "the
captivity of things." For such men, as he saw it, the
evangelical life was the natural mode of existence.

There was no choice for Francis but to accept the
new Rule.

But that sad event was still two years away during

the winter of 1220–1 spent by him at Portiuncula.
The coming of spring of 1221 brought Francis refreshment and an increase of physical strength. In
the early summer of 1221 he left Umbria for Rome.
Ugolino's summons to a man who no longer wielded
authority was not as surprising as it may appear.

Pietro di Catana had died in March 1221, and
Elias of Cortona had succeeded him, although no
chapter had been summoned for the election. The
affairs of the Order were in another's hands, but
Ugolino knew well that Francis still remained the
heartbeat, and the Cardinal, having formed a scheme
for the recruitment of Dominicans and Franciscans
into the ranks of episcopacy, felt that he could not
carry it out without a consultation with Francis and
Dominic. The latter said that it seemed to him that
the missionary work of his sons, together with their
teaching at the universities, would never leave enough
leisure for diocesan matters. Francis replied that he
no longer had any authority to form judgments, but
the Cardinal pressed him to give his opinion.

"The friars," answered the little man, "are still
called '*minores*,' and they should never become '*majores*' as they would be if they carried croziers. If you
wish them to do good in the Church, leave them
alone."

Francis might well have added, "if such a thing is
at all possible."

The image of the Lady Poverty, her feet bare and
her clothes tattered, had become more than patchily
blurred for many among the Brothers Minor. "The
House of Friars" at Bologna no longer excited anyone's curiosity. Provincial ministers lived in houses
openly belonging to the Order. Such properties being

taxable, the administration had to deal with large sums of money. The novitiate ended and the final vows taken, a brother would indeed give up all he possessed down to a pair of broken shoes, but those possessions now passed into the communal keeping and were not distributed among the poor. Some of the young men who felt that they were called to the Franciscan life were either heirs or owners of large properties which, once handed over to the Order, had to be managed by properly appointed obedientaries. It was all strictly legal and in perfect accord with the prevailing usage. Now, scholars were told to continue their studies, and many friars were held in high honor at the universities in Italy, and beyond the Alps. The biannual chapters were still held at Portiuncula, but the earlier Franciscan spirit had gone out of them.

By 1223, the great cleft deepened between the Conventuals on one side and the Strict Observants on the other. Yet, the unhappy division notwithstanding, both parties still considered Francis as their spiritual head.

And he was conscious of it. He remained himself to the very end, a faithful knight of his Lord and of the Lady Poverty, invariably courteous and gay even when his mind was shrouded by sadness. Great numbers of his sons were reluctant to accept the 1223 Rule so poignantly out of accord with the original idea, and Francis never censured them for their reluctance. On occasions he even encouraged it. He knew that some of the friars were ashamed of the spreading use of the word "mine," and that many others were irked by the narrowly grooved trivia of the daily life now imposed on them.

One German friar tramped across the Alps into

Umbria at a time when the Strict Observants were
almost at the edge of a revolt against the Conventuals.
At Portiuncula, the German said to Francis:

"Father, I ask one favor of you. If all the brothers
ever come to cease leading a life of poverty, will you
let me and other friars in my country abandon them
and observe the Rule wholly?" And at those words,
as his biographers tell us, "Francis felt a great joy,"
and replied: "Christ and I authorize what you have
asked for," an answer wholly unconcerned with any
"legality."

In Umbria, at least, the Strict Observants did not
lose heart—however anxious they were. Brother Leo,
for one, came to Portiuncula "to open his mind" to
Francis. Later, the little man wrote to him: "I reply,
yes, my son. This word sums up all we said whilst
walking together. . . . Whatever may be the manner
in which you think to please the Lord God, follow
it and live in poverty. Do this, God will bless you,
and I authorize it. And if it were necessary for your
soul and your comfort to come and see me again, or
if you wish it, my Leo, come,"—a short enough letter
but wholly informed by the spirit of liberty taught by
Francis from the very beginning.

Elias of Cortona worked in perfect accord with
the Roman Curia, and all the provincial ministers
were responsible to him alone. One of the greatest
religious orders had started its work in every corner
of Christendom, and its members would certainly
realize many of Ugolino's earliest hopes. But could
they truly claim Francis for their founder?

Yet, both the claim and its negation lack relevancy.
To found world-wide organizations was not Francis'

mission. To bring "the joy of the Lord" into innumerable dark lives was the cornerstone of his apostolate, and there he certainly did not fail either in his own day or later.

The Holy La...

mission. To bring "the joy of the Lord" into innumerable dark lives was the cornerstone of his
apostolate, and his apostolate did not fail either
in his own day or later.

CHAPTER NINE

THE HAPPY PURITANS

CHRONOLOGICALLY, the movement here described
does belong to the year 1221 when Rome granted
official recognition to the Franciscan Tertiaries, i.e.,
men and women of all social degrees who, without
leaving the world for the cloister, became members of
the Third Order. But the bull of Honorius III (*Sig-
nificatum est*, dated December 16, 1221) did little
more than put the official seal on a movement con-
temporaneous with Francis' apostolate. So, in a wider
sense, would be the Tertiaries' Rule promulgated in
1289 by Pope Nicholas IV, Minister-General of the
Brothers Minor before his elevation to the papal
throne.

Even Francis' enemies, who spared no efforts to
disparage everything said and done by him, had to
admit, however reluctantly, that his preaching possessed a quality which carried his hearers away. It
was not the mere content of his sermons since there
was nothing original in them. It was not tricks and
gestures of an experienced popular preacher determined to win attention by studied whispers or shouts,
by the rolling of eyes, and the twisting of fingers.
Such pulpit tricks were alien to Francis. Rather, it
was the burden of his message which, however art-
lessly delivered, struck novel chords in the hearers'
consciousness: God loved the world and the people
living in it. Let them grieve for their sins and then

rise in joy because of the abundant beauty they saw. And Francis would speak as an intimate of the Lord, himself wholly unconscious of the intimacy. It was precisely his "joy in the Lord" that carried contagion. He was like someone who, given a beautiful present, cannot wholly enjoy it unless or until his entire acquaintance be given an opportunity to share in his delight. Thus, in a sense, the birthday of the Third Order may well have coincided with Francis' very first sermons at Assisi.

Yet, neither reliable sources nor legends so much as hint at it. It is Celano in his Life who enables us to see that the Third Order came into being because of enthusiasm among the Umbrians on Francis' return from Rome in 1210, and Celano's account is borne out by other sources. *The Book of the Three Companions* mentions it and, according to the *Fioretti* (*The Little Flowers*), it was at Saburniano, not far from Bevagna, that "[Francis] bethought him of the Third Order which he established," the same Saburniano which, together with his companions, the little Umbrian reached "taking heed of neither road nor path . . ." and there he preached in the open, near a well, and left ". . . the people much comforted and truly disposed to penitence." During the same journey from Rome, Francis made a halt at Rieti, and ". . . he tarried there because of the great harvest of souls gathered from among the people who came to listen to him." Elsewhere, as we are told, "He preached what the Holy Spirit taught him, and so wondrously that he seemed to speak with the voice of an angel rather than of a man. His words pierced many hearts like arrows."

Now, Francis was then returning from Rome, his first mission, as he believed, ended triumphantly. He had gained friends in high places, but that was not the main reason for his happy mood. He had been listened to by the Vicar of Christ and was returning to Umbria, a papal blessing on his labors. His companions were exultant. So was Francis, for once determined not to see a single cloud in his sky. Far too intelligent not to perceive that Rome had not understood his aims, far too loyal a Catholic to doubt the sincerity of a Pope's promise, Francis was coming home, joy possessing him. There were many halts along the journey. He preached everywhere, for how could he keep silent about his joy?

In *The Little Flowers of St. Francis* we have a story of one such halt, and the name of the place is not given. It may have been a village or a small town. It must have been in a plain because there was a castle "on the top of the hill." Once there, Francis preached "strongly and fierily" against vicious living, and "all manner of ungodliness and its dread reward in the hereafter." That done, his theme turned to calmer waters. "Be sorry. . . . Resolve not to sin again. Invite the Lord into your homes and hearts." And what was to come after? The joy, the peace, the liberty of a soul loosed from the dark prison of sin and self into the fragrant radiance of the Lord's garden.

Francis could say such things because he had lived them. They were more real to him than the dust under his bare feet. And, at that unnamed place, he spoke of them with heightened vigor and sharpened awareness.

The people heard him. According to the contem-

porary evidence, they were "stirred from their sleep."
From the castle and the village, the entire population
surrounded the little man. The lord and his swineherd
stood together. The lady's ladies and the peasants'
wives were shoulder to shoulder. The elegantly
dressed pages and the lads who helped the goatherds
were there in a closer proximity than had ever been
imagined. The armed guards from the castle and the
cowmen in their rags were there, all welded together
in a strange urge. Francis had finished, and they surrounded him until he could not move—so thick was
the press on his right hand and on his left. From the
lord of the castle down to the cowman, they were all
weeping, gesturing, shouting that they were ready to
renounce the world and to follow the Lord. Francis'
words had enflamed them, and they wished the fire
would consume them and put an end to all the complications of their daily lives.

They were a crowd, and we cannot tell how Francis' companions responded to such a turbulent reaction. We know how Francis met it.

He did not rebuke them. He did not tell them they
were mad. Nor did he send them away empty-handed.
He told them the Lord would have no joy in broken
homes and disrupted lives. We are told that "he
calmed the multitude," no easy task for a tired man.
Obviously, Francis and his companions did not spend
the night at that place because we hear of "a multitude
following them beyond the gates." And there the little
man turned, faced the crowd, and told them to turn
back. "Stay in your homes—and I promise to find a
way for you all to serve God."

The promise was made at a certain place on a

certain day. The beginning might almost be called provincial; in Francis' day Italian communities, whatever their size and importance, were extremely jealous of their independence often enough wrested at a high cost to life and property. The scene described above was built on the record left by eyewitnesses. The lord of the castle and his ragged swineherd, the innkeeper and the beggar, velvet cloaks and coarsely spun tunics, ease and hardship, sinful plenty and no less wicked penury, "all sorts and conditions" of men, women, and, so we are told, children, were included within a gesture of charity. Some among them rushed into extravagant promises: there were wives all but ready to leave their husbands for the love of God, merchants prepared to pledge themselves to abandon trade and to start on a pilgrimage, farmers and peasants willing to forsake flocks and fields. All those had their answer. "Stay where you are—do what you were doing, and I will not forget my promise."

Out of that incident a new leaven was born to spread not only all over Italy and Europe, but far beyond.

At the beginning those men and women were not known as Tertiaries but as Brothers and Sisters of Penitence, the last word applied in a strictly Franciscan sense. "The Lord's beggar" did not expect those people to devote themselves to obvious penitential labors. His friars were carrying on with God's work in the spirit of cheerfulness and joyfulness. These, Francis' larger family, had their pattern given to them within the same framework. They were to work for peace. They promised not to take up arms except in those cases when imminent danger threatened their country. Before their admission into the family, both men and women were expected to forgive and forget all the injuries done to them in the past, to make peace with all their enemies, and not to harbor hatred in their thoughts for the future. Brothers and Sisters were also urged to abstain from litigation, that nursery bed of so much bitterness and even violence during the period, and they had to abandon the familiar idea that insults could be blotted out by revenge.

Since they remained in the world, their service of the Lady Poverty must inevitably be qualified. They could not be expected to give everything away—but ill-gotten gains had to be surrendered on admission. They were expected to practice the spirit of poverty as widely as their condition allowed, to spend very little on personal adornment and luxuries, and not to indulge in expensive entertainment. Francis urged them to find the utmost vocational value in the tiniest circumstances of their daily life. Rooms could be dusted, trees felled, embroidery made, account books kept, cattle and horses watered, beans cooked and eaten, a patch put on a garment, and rushlight lit to the glory of the Lord. Those Brothers and Sisters were asked to use anything they possessed as if they were stewards and not owners. At the time of their admission they promised to keep God's commandments "during the entire course of their lives."

They were not to be distinguished by their dress except insofar as it was not extravagant, but they could be buried in the brown smock such as the friars wore. Portiuncula remained their spiritual harbor, and prayers of the fellowship companioned them through life and beyond it.

Francis did not burden them with devotions which

would have encroached upon their ordinary work.
Nothing was asked of them over and above the normal
Christian practices of Mass and Sacraments except for
the recital of eight Paternosters, followed by a Gloria,
for each of the eight canonical hours, i.e., Matins,
Lauds, Prime, Terce, Sext, None, Vespers, and
Compline. Church bells told those hours, and people
were accustomed to shape the day's work in accordance with them. In his choice of the Lord's Prayer,
Francis once again proved himself a man of genius.
The majority of Brothers and Sisters were illiterate.
To find their way in and out of the complexities of
the Breviary would have been wholly beyond them.
Not so "Our Father," a firm anchor of a prayer known
to them all since their childhood days; and its brief
paraphrase found among Francis' writings, which
begins "Most Holy Father" ("*Sanctissime Pater*"),
its date rather uncertain, may well have been composed for some among the first members of his "larger
family."

All in all, it seemed a road of charity, liberty, and
responsibility open to all.

It is impossible to overemphasize its importance
for the people of Francis' generation. It was an abso-
lutely novel departure in the medieval world. The
whole purpose of life in this world was the salvation
of one's soul. The laity stumbled towards that goal as
best they could. If they were moneyed folk, they bequeathed large sums to the Church for Masses,
candles and prayers to shorten their stay in Purgatory
and to assure their entrance into Paradise. But everybody knew that by far the surer way to salvation lay
through the cloister gate.

And here was Francis urging that lay folk could lead a hallowed life while still in the world, that it was not necessary for everybody to leave the world, that anyone could follow his profession or business, however humble, and belong wholly to God, and that it did not matter a tittle if a man was a count or a beggar, if a woman was a highborn lady or a beggar's wife accustomed to bearing babies in a ditch. For, to Francis, all "were children of the same Father." Those first Tertiaries might well be called the vanguard of European democracies. They answered the Umbrian's challenge with unbridled enthusiasm at first. As time went on, the wild flame burned brightly but steadily, and nothing would ever extinguish it.

When Clare and her first followers were established at San Damiano, Francis realized that there he had a most rewarding focal point for the Umbrian Sisters of Penitence. Clare's robust common sense, her loyalty, her deep understanding of his aims and, above all, her shining spirituality made of her an ideal counselor for the women and girls about to join the Third Order. The buildings at San Damiano were small, but there were the grounds, and the mild climate allowed of nights spent in the open through the better part of the year.

According to tradition, the first to join that lay Franciscan family were one Luca of Gianzi in the neighborhood of Siena, his wife, Bona, and a Roman nobleman, one Matteo de Rubeo, father of a future Pope, Nicholas IV.

Luca's story well illustrates Francis' influence on those who listened to him for the first time.

Still in his twenties, Luca was a corn merchant

known even beyond his immediate neighborhood for
his stoniness of heart. From his father he had inherited a sizable fortune in land and money and
rapidly increased it by methods which, without vio-
lating the law of the state, were certainly against the
law of God. Luca's large funds enabled him to buy
up grain stocks all over Umbria. He would hoard the
supplies until a bad harvest played into his hands.
Then Luca would bring the hoarded grain to the market and sell it at an iniquitous profit. The well-to-do
people grumbled and cursed him but they paid the
price. The poor folk starved, a matter of indifference
to Luca. He would invest his ill-gotten gains in more
and more land, farm it out most advantageously, and
prosper and grow fat in his prosperity. Bona was
very proud of her husband. The local clergy were far
too pusillanimous to interfere, still less to rebuke the
transgressor—all the more so because, his meanness
notwithstanding, Luca hoped that occasional gifts of
money, corn, wine, and wax would pave his way to
the gates of Paradise.

We do not know exactly where Luca first heard
Francis preach, but it seems as though there was no
immediate dramatic resolvement. Vaguely enough
the corn merchant sensed that a great many wrongs
lay at his door, but he was not prompted to make any
public admission. His granaries were full to bursting,
his many farms yielding fair returns, and he was no
thief in reality. Bad harvests were none of his doing.

Nonetheless, Luca felt disquieted. He went home
and told his wife: "The little beggar looks mean
and insignificant, but something in his words has
burned into me, and I have no wish to burn in

Eternity." Bona, being a practical woman, decided
to go and hear Francis herself. On returning home,
she said briefly, "Come, let us see the holy man together. You were right about his words. They burn
you."

Hand in hand, husband and wife reached the field
where Francis was still preaching. Then Bona took
off all her bangles and buckles and laid them at the
little man's feet, and both Luca and she asked to be
received into the family.

All the lands and farms were given away, and the
vast stocks of hoarded grain distributed to the poor.
Luca kept nothing except one house, a small garden,
and an ass. The house was turned into a hospice for
the homeless and the sick, and Luca, with the ass for
his companion, took to searching for "new friends"
in the highways and byways. Once a sufferer was
found, Luca would hoist him on the ass's back and
return home where Bona would nurse the man. The
small garden provided them with fruit, herbs, and
vegetables. Luca of Gianzi considered himself fortunate indeed to be a sharer in "the joy of the Lord."

The story may well have gathered a few legendary
touches in the course of several retellings, but it
affords a striking illustration of Francis' power over
his listeners.

So, little by little, the laity were drawn into the
family. The tide, having spread over Umbria and
Tuscany, swept northward and southward. We know
that after his return from the Holy Land, Francis
attempted no further journeys abroad, and that his
missionary labors were confined to Italy. His biographers tell us that he was said to preach in as many as

five villages during a single day—whenever the state of his health allowed it. Soon, groups of Brothers and Sisters coalesced into definite communities and were given in charge of so-called "Visitors" chosen from among the friars. The hierarchy, beginning with Cardinal Ugolino, soon realized the great spiritual worth of the new departure. Kings and Queens all over Europe sought for admission. St. Louis of France and St. Elizabeth of Hungary belonged to the Third Order, to cite but two great names.

Ramifications, changes, and many rather saddening formalities, however, were still to come at the time when Francis went about his Lord's business. Having laid the foundation stone, as it were, he left the rest to God. That he once again brought a fresh breath into so many clogged lives probably never would have occurred to him. That his newly recruited Brothers and Sisters formed the vanguard of a spiritually quickened democracy is again an idea which would never have found lodgment in his mind.

It was enough for him to see more and more men and women freed from "the captivity of things," and enabled to serve their Maker within their newly acquired liberty.

Portiuncula became the Tertiaries' cradle and San Damiano their harbor. They were truly of the family —but they stood aloof from all the administrative matters. The labors of the Franciscan apostolate were not for them, committed as they were to all the normal avocations of their daily life. Hence, the thickening dissensions within the Order did not really affect them.

Their mode of life is reflected in the title to this

chapter. They were certainly the Puritans of the
thirteenth century—they spent very little on themselves, they were frugal at table and did not get
drunk, they did not frequent public entertainments
which at the time would end in drunken brawls and
worse, and they wore soberly colored clothes. But
none of it made for pious gloom in their daily lives.
You would not have recognized an early Tertiary by
a long face, set lips, a mournful expression in the
eyes, and a general disapproval of the most fugitive
ray of sunshine across the sky. They were truly Francis' sons and daughters in their consciousness of "the
joy of the Lord."

Theirs was a leaven which, once entering the
Christian climate, never left it altogether.

CHAPTER TEN

JERUSALEM IN UMBRIA

EVEN today there remain some wild places in Italy, hard of access, savagely beautiful, and assured of a privacy never to be violated by the intrusion of man's all too often clumsily fashioned contrivances—a rocky bluff, a generously wide shelf of mountain grown all over with thick-girthed trees, the loud anger of a waterfall heard from a distance and the undertones of an unseen rill, some twisting steep path ending at the edge of a surprising patch of even, emerald-green ground, encircled by juniper and tamarisk, suggesting a plate of rare majolica offered on the palm of Atlas—narrow ribbons of tracks threading up and down, pine needles for their carpet and skies for their roof—not a single evidence of any human habitation but the pulse of life beating richly in tree and water, in birdsong and the unseen footfall of animals, and the majesty of mountain peaks most surprisingly in accord with the tiny pink and blue flowers edging the track.

In such places, recorded history becomes less than a crumb of a loaf. The earth does not so much belong to man as man to earth. Whether he will or no, he stands subject to the natural law and may, if he so chooses, come to a sense of a curious release by virtue of the subjection. However wild the landscape, it is informed by a truth seldom found elsewhere. Also it promises an enlargement of horizons other than the visible one.

In the thirteenth century there were many more such places all over the peninsula.

Some time between 1213 and 1215, Francis, accompanied by Brother Leo, happened to be in the neighborhood of Montefeltro when a great festivity was going on at the castle. There Francis preached, taking no text but a popular rhyme for the opening words:

> *Tanto é il bene ch'iō aspetto*
> *ch' ogni pena m'é diletto.*

("So great a good I wait for that any hardship is a delight.")

"So movingly and strongly did [Francis] preach on that occasion that people listened as though he were an angel of God," says Celano, who doubtless recorded it from the eyewitness account of Brother Leo. Among the hearers was a very wealthy young man, Count Orlando di Chiusi in Casentino. So struck was he by Francis' sermon that he sought him out and talked of "weighty matters" with the little Umbrian. In the end, the young Count joined the Third Order. Also he wished to make some return to Francis for all the help so generously given. Orlando recognized Francis' need for occasional spells of solitude in between the apostolic journeys. The Count offered a most imaginative gift, and Francis accepted it gladly: a thickly wooded peak in the Apennines, known as Monte Verna, so hard to reach that its privacy was unlikely ever to be broken.

Monte Verna was in Casentino, a region so richly sheltered by nature that the thunders of invasions, let alone civil strife, had always spared it. Girdled by high mountains on every side, offering neither pass nor path to any inimical alien, its tiny villages and hamlets studded along rocky shelves, Casentino bred hard-mettled people, unafraid of what few strangers found the way into their fastnesses. Walled in by stupendous rocks and sheltered from tempests, the region enjoyed a mild climate and prosperity, too, with its vineyards, olive and mulberry trees, and orchards. The woods abounded in pine, chestnut, beech, and oak. The waters were rich in fish, and never had the promise of harvest been destroyed by the tramp of mailed feet.

Monte Verna reared its peak between the sources of the Tiber and the Arno on the very borders of Tuscany. The mountain looked majestic but not forbidding. Its slopes were thickly wooded with great clearances here and there. All through the spring and early summer, the ground was enameled with violets, pink and white hepatica, anemones, wild narcissi, and cyclamen. Birdsong deepened the peace. From the summit, reached by the mere hint of a precipitous track, both the Mediterranean and the Adriatic could be seen. To the south lay the smiling valley of Umbria.

Count di Chiusi's men had built a few rough huts for the friars on one of the middle slopes facing east, and Monte Verna became one of the many hermitages. Together with a few companions, Francis would occasionally spend some days there during his travels between Umbria and the north. He had loved the place from the very beginning. In 1224, the longing for its peace grew sharper than ever.

It was a thorny year for him. Not a day but would be fretted with anxieties about the future of the

Order. The cleft between the Conventuals and the Strict Observants was widening. There had even been flashes of violence, particularly on the part of the former. In such troubled shallows, the fair image of charity grew more and more blurred.

Dominic was dead. Ugolino remained a friend and a sorrow. However obvious his affection for and sympathy with Francis, the Cardinal could not help following a policy, its drift wholly alien to the little man's ideals. The Rule of 1223, solemnly confirmed by Honorius III, had, as it were, put shoes on the Lady Poverty's beautiful feet and clothed her with a raiment she should never have worn. Elias of Cortona ruled the Order, and his vicars, far more than two in number, administered the provinces in a manner which saddened and irked the Strict Observants. There were expenses and revenues, their volume swelling every year. Brothers Minor owned houses and lands not only in Italy but far beyond the Alps. They preached incessantly. They also studied—particularly in Paris and Bologna. No episcopal interference now harassed them—they had been given far too many privileges by the Roman Curia.

They had certainly won their place in the Catholic sun and that in spite of the battle raging between the two camps. The cleft notwithstanding, the Founder still remained the heartbeat, Portiuncula stood for a Franciscan cradle, and Clare at San Damiano remained faithful to her profession. Yet all was far from well with Francis. Doubts, anguish, sleepless nights, wracking headaches, an increasing weakness of the limbs together with a growing pain in his eyes, such was his portion. San Damiano and

Portiuncula, where his loyal intimates still spoke a language he could understand, those were the only stars in Francis' sky through that storm-tossed period. He made no protests to the Conventuals who came to visit him, but he felt himself wholly forsaken. Even his hours of prayer became a torment which would be eased by nothing except an intensified meditation on the Passion. There, Francis felt, he might some day find his way into the climate of reconciliation and see some light thrown upon what he considered his failure to interpret God's love for man.

His nights became tunnels of horror. Wracked by insomnia, Francis would time and again fall prey to demoniac attacks. The same finely veined sensibility which had been the source of much delight, now gave birth to one terror after another.

It is now fashionable to deny the Devil and all his works, and from one point of view those tribulations of Francis' might seem so many chimerae born out of an uncontrolled imagination. Nothing could have been further from reality. Even an average believer in God, his spiritual consciousness developed none too deeply, must admit that to deny the existence of evil is tantamount to providing another triumph for evil. And in Francis we have no average Christian but a flaming spiritual genius, his mystic intuition making him shape his course toward "the Delectable Mountains" of a true mystic's vision, i.e., union with God. He was enabled to feel God's Presence on all his pulses, and for some years his constant prayer had been to be given a share in Christ's cup. Christ had been tempted, and so was Francis.

Through those sleepless nights the demons crowded

outside his door and invaded his cell. The rushlight Francis occasionally allowed himself would flicker and go out, and he would find himself in a hideously peopled dark. Within it, the shining beauty of his ideal was fouled by the trampling of cloven feet. Concentrated evil, assuming shapes he could recognize all too well, hissed and spat at the Lady Poverty, spat at him, and rained blows upon his body. He would try to pray for deliverance, but evil crowded into the cell, strangled his capacity for prayer. He heard more hissing and louder laughter. Above the fiendish cacophony, the sense of absolute failure reared itself, a monstrous hammer threatening to fall upon his soul.

Such, then, were some of Francis' experiences, each detail perfectly in accord with his apprehension of demoniac faculties. The blows and kicks falling on his body were no more imaginary than, say, the wrenching of a picture from a wall by a poltergeist's agency.

At last he came to a decision, and Clare was glad to hear of it.

Physically, Francis needed a rest, but he needed a spiritual quietening even more. In the past, that might have been granted him during a mission. Such labors were beyond him at the time. So, when the tempest had briefly receded, Francis decided to go into a long retreat. He would keep what he called "Michaelmas Lent," i.e., from Assumption Day until the 29th of September, and he thought it would be best kept on Monte Verna. He loved Portiuncula—but the place was no longer a real hermitage. Too many people came there for comfort and counsel. True, the friars knew that Francis' health did not always permit him to see visitors, but their arrival alone would trouble him. Once he knew that any stranger wished to see him, Francis could not refuse. A headache all but blinding him, he would see the guest with his habitual courtesy, listen patiently, and send the man away comforted.

Again, Portiuncula was too close to Assisi. Far too many Assisians, now firmly convinced that Francis was their very own saint, would bring their problems to his cell. Nobleman or beggar, Francis denied none of them. They were his own dear people.

Finally, any friar returning to "the cradle" from a mission might all too easily deepen the day's grief with his stories of yet another conflict between the Conventuals and the Strict Observants, or yet another property either acquired by, or bequeathed to, the Order. They felt it was only right for their Father to learn of such things, and he did not reproach them for selfishness, but it certainly added to the load he was carrying. All in all, Portiuncula, however cherished, was no place for the kind of retreat he had in mind.

He had hoped to start for Monte Verna early in July. His physical condition did not permit it. He bore the delay with his habitual cheerfulness.

Brothers Leo, Angelo, and Masseo were to be his companions. Such was Francis' weakness that the three men wondered if he would reach Monte Verna alive. He yielded to their pleas that he should ride a donkey throughout the journey. Even so, they must make a great number of halts and ministered to Francis as much as he allowed them. When near to the mountain, they stopped for the last time and

helped Francis to dismount. He made his way slowly
to the shade of an old oak and lay down on the ground,
his eyes closed.

Suddenly, as his companions would later record,
". . . a multitude of birds began singing overhead, . . ." and, presently, winging low, they took to
perching all over Francis. He lay very still, and the
friars were happy to see him smile.

"This is our welcome to Monte Verna," he told
them, "and could we have hoped for a better one?"

Soon, they reached the hermitage where Francis
had a tiny separate hut at the foot of "a very fair
beech." But he would not keep his Lent there. On
the eve of Assumption Day he withdrew to a barely
accessible cave on the southern side of Monte Verna.
Brother Leo alone was permitted to bring him what
very few necessities were needed—a little bread and
a handful of vegetables, and even such a meager
ration was not brought every day. For his companions
Francis had many birds, in particular a falcon which
had her nest close to the cave's entrance.

Leo, Masseo, and Angelo were alike disturbed by
Francis' withdrawal—chiefly because of his physical
frailty; but presently they persuaded themselves that
he would be as much in God's care in that cave as
anywhere else in the world, and there would be
Brother Leo to bring them any messages Francis
chose to send them. They prepared to spend their
own long vigil as best they knew—in prayer, meditation, fishing, and gathering what wild berries and
roots grew in the neighborhood. When they did not
keep silence, they talked about things best answering
the climate of an absolute retreat. They never dis-

cussed the matters of the Order. The tumult of the
world had no part in that place.

On the way from Portiuncula, Francis had sometimes talked with his three friends about his death.
For several months his thoughts had been occupied
with the Passion in a very particular way. Now, alone
on that southern slope of Monte Verna, his absorption
became complete. He indeed carried the book of the
Gospels with him, but there was no need for him
to turn to those pages: the story was known to his
inmost heart. By now Francis' memory was enriched
by the remembered scenes of the Palestinian landscape, the folds of the little hills, the small olive
groves, the clusters of fig trees by the roadside, many
customs unchanged since the days of the patriarchs.
The skies over the Holy Land had been seen by him,
and he had heard the ripples of a quiet lake—never
to forget them.

The believer in Francis considered all those memories; deep humility and silent adoration possessed
him. The knight in him was prompted once again to
offer his service to the Lord of all chivalry in Christendom. The poet in him turned to the evocative power
which enabled him to see images ranging from
dazzling light to midnight darkness.

The world of Francis' generation teemed with
relics, some of them genuine enough, a great many
faked out of men's greed. What he had found in
Palestine, and what his faith and love once again
held closest of all, was no sumptuously bejeweled
reliquary but a living truth—just as the Four Gospels
stood for far more than words written on parchment.

Francis was no scholar, but he had been to Spain,

and a Spanish saint's prayer may well have been known to him. Those lines are given here because they express the entire mood of Francis' long vigil on Monte Verna—and his passionate longing for a share in Christ's travail, not for his own enrichment, but for the sake of the world.

> I come to thee in the great humility of my spirit; and I shall speak to thee because of the great hope and strength thou hast given me. O thou, son of David, who camest to us in the flesh, open the secret of my heart with the nail of thy Cross. Send down one of thy seraphim to cleanse my lips with the burning coal from thy altar and to uncloud my mind that the tongue which tries to serve my neighbor by charity, may never speak in error but may never cease to sing the praises of truth.[1]

Again, one line of a great Passion hymn which Francis would often have sung in processions up and down the streets of Assisi endorses the purpose of that long retreat: *"Fulget Crucis mysterium"*— "The secret of the Cross doth shine."[2]

---

[1] The text is in Migne, *Patrologia Latina*, Vol. 96. Julian, Archbishop of Toledo (sixth to seventh centuries) can hardly be called a voluminous author, but some of the pieces left by him are fine indeed. He was a scholar and a great gardener. The prayer quoted, called *"Oratio Iulianis,"* was included in the Mozarabic Liturgy and recited by the priest after the washing of hands during Mass.

[2] This is the second line of the hymn *"Vexilla Regis prodeunt"* ("The Royal Banners forward go"). Its author, Venantius Fortunatus—Bishop of Poitiers—was neither saint nor mystic, but he had his great moments. Queen Radegund,

An unshrouded mystery is a paradox. In bald
terms, it carries no meaning at all. But the secret of
the Cross could—and did—burn with a dazzling
light. Something lived within that mystery which
turned it into a bridge to link the darkness of
Gethsemane and Golgotha to a spring garden in the
morning and an empty tomb.

Towards some such goal had Francis striven ever
since the day of his conversion. Its challenge would
now recede, now come nearer, its compulsion never
leaving him altogether. During the journey to Monte
Verna, the objective grew less and less faint. So
profoundly did he reflect upon the union of joy and
triumph with sorrow and loss that his Master and he
could hardly have stood closer to each other.

Now, alone in that cave, Francis was being drawn
nearer and nearer to the reality at once within and
behind the Passion. Expressions such as "once in
Galilee" would have been meaningless to him since
there was no longer any sense of time in his thought.
He, the Lord's *"joculator,"* the gay, laughing, and

Abbess of St. Cross at Poitiers, was his friend and patroness.
Towards the end of the sixth century, the Emperor of
Byzantium, having heard much of her piety, sent a relic of
the True Cross for her abbey, and the Queen asked Venantius
to mark the occasion in a manner best answering his genius.
He wrote four Passion hymns sung during the ceremonies
surrounding the coming of the relic to Poitiers. In the second
line of the *Vexilla Regis* Venantius stumbled on a splendor.
Centuries later, the line *"Fulget Crucis mysterium"* was
Englished most ineptly as "The Cross shines forth in mystic
glow." It never occurred to the translator that the entire
meaning of the line rests upon the noun *mysterium* being
linked with the verb *fulget* (shines), and not the other
way about.

singing apostle, whose very gravity would seldom be tinged with soberness, was now being drawn nearer and nearer to the little hill outside the gates of Jerusalem, all his faculties plunging deeper and deeper into the secret of sorrow, and reaching towards the splendors beyond. Finally, Francis reached a point when even a fleeting glance at his crucifix would evoke a response to unite the night of the soul with a sunrise never to know a setting.

It was the most daring and stupendous spiritual travail. It taxed his faith to the uttermost since, together with Christ's disciples, Francis had to approach Good Friday, his mind and soul shuttered even from a distant glimpse of the Empty Tomb. Once having asked for the grace of sharing in the Passion, he could not expect to be spared the anguish of "My God, my God, why hast thou forsaken me?" Little enough, if anything, would be told his companions when the vigil was ended. Most likely, human language lacked the words fit to interpret that experience. It certainly seared Francis to the uttermost. In terms of hard logic, it should have stripped him of what few shreds of strength were still his. But it did not do so. That constant meditation upon the Passion raised Francis from one nightfall to another. It strengthened all his spiritual and mental sinews. It taught him that doubt and anguish were just so many futile attitudes and reminded him of what he should never have forgotten—that despair was a sin against the Holy Spirit. It ended by reconciling Francis to what he still thought was his failure. On Monte Verna, *il Poverello* was indeed stripped, and yet never before had he been clad so richly. God's love had woven him a garment to endure for Eternity.

Assumption falls on August 15. The fourteenth
of September is the Feast of the Exaltation of the
Cross, and in the Middle Ages it was considered as
one of the finest jewels in the liturgical calendar. It
was the patronal festival of the crusaders, some of
whom Francis had met and over whose lapses he had
wept. Yet such matters ceased to concern him now.
"And I, if I be lifted up on the cross. . . ." To him,
the words carried an immediacy nobody could challenge. What mattered his own infinitesimal failure in
the face of such a triumph?

He had spent a whole month by himself, but he
had lost all reckoning of Time—now become of less
import than an oak leaf driven hither and thither at
the whim of an autumn gale. Below, in the hermitage,
Leo, Angelo, and Masseo knew that their father was
praying for the grace of the greatest share possible
in the Master's grief. They knew no more than that.
Even Brother Leo, "the little sheep" and closest con-
fidant, would not have dared to intrude with an
immoment question.

We cannot tell if Francis had ever read St. Bernard, but certainly Francis belonged to that very
small company of men and women able not only to
grasp the meaning but to live the reality of St. Bernard's words in the treatise "On the Love of God":
"*Causa diligendi Deum: Deus est. Modus—sine modo
diligere*"—i.e., "the reason for loving God is that God
exists. The measure of that love should be without
measure."[3]

---

[3] I offer my apologies for the somewhat free rendering of
the second sentence, but the scholastic term "*modus*," if
literally translated, rather chills the meaning of the whole.

At sunset of September 13, 1224, Francis left the cave and made for a small clearing in a wood at no great distance from the hermitage. There he spent his last vigil. He was scarcely conscious of his body. Through those hours, of whose passing he could not have been aware, everything was stilled within him and without.

Just before dawn Francis turned eastward—to where the Adriatic lay, whose waters he could not see. But the world he saw was being renewed, and he realized that he held his share in the newness. The grayness began breaking away; the East glowed with washes of faint lemon-green radiance, and gradually, the hesitant light spread and grew stronger to spill its glory over bare rocks, trees, and water. Held very still within that newness, Francis saw the shape of a seraph flying towards him, the six wings outspread, gleaming rose-silver against the golden air. The vision drew nearer and nearer until Francis could see that the shining wings were nailed to a cross. He looked on and on until the light absorbed the vision wholly. At that very moment, his ecstasy was mingled with an excruciating physical pain. He looked down and saw the marks of nails on his palms and a small wound gleaming red in his left side. And his feet hurt him.

It was an agony he had never imagined to exist. The pain gripped him wholly, but its very essence seemed linked to a joy beyond his comprehension. Good Friday and the Resurrection morning were at one in Time and in Eternity, the midnight desolation of Calvary enlarging and deepening the triumph of Easter. Within that vastness, beyond all measure

known to man, Francis' efforts, failure, and achieve-
ment became as nought. He was less than a grain of
sand upon the seashore. Yet, he was greater than the
Seraphim because he had read the secret of Christ's
humanity, and within his own manhood Francis was
one with the Son of God.

It was a secret, and he would treat it as such. He
had truly been in Gethsemane, on Calvary, and in the
garden with Pilate's guards keeping watch over the
tomb. But such things could not be told even to his
intimates.

The goal so long prayed for was reached. Francis
knew that his nature was changed into the likeness
of the Crucified Who rose from the dead and showed
the way to Eternity.

Then physical exhaustion took its toll. Francis fell,
his face to the ground.

Such, then, was the outward pattern of the vision
and its consequence as recorded by those few with
whom Francis would share what he could of the most
sublime experience ever fallen to a Christian's lot. He
had long hoped for a martyrdom. Now he was sealed
to Christ, united with Him through the love-lit reality
of the Passion—at once a secret and a revelation of
God's care for man.

A little later, Brother Leo, coming to the cave to
leave the day's meager ration at the entrance, was
greeted by the falcon. He peered inside. The cave
was empty, and the faithful friar's heart was filled
with forebodings. He started searching, and it was
some time before he came on Francis still prostrate
on the ground. But he was fully conscious and turned

on hearing Leo's steps. "The little sheep" was
amazed "by the joy and serenity" of Francis' look. He
tried to get up and walk, but the pierced soles made
the least movement so difficult that he sank back to
the ground, and Leo hurried off to summon Masseo
and Angelo.

Presently, the three friars carried Francis down to
the hermitage, and busied themselves with preparing
a meal, their awe all but engulfing their affection.
They had seen his hands and feet and took note of
the crimson stain on the left side of the tunic. They
asked no questions. When the pottage was ready,
they brought the bowl to Francis, who did not refuse
the food. A little later, he charged his three friends
to keep silent about what they had seen.

At this point of Francis' story, the following facts
are apposite enough to merit insertion.

The authenticity of *il Poverello*'s autograph, preserved at Assisi, has long been established. It is a
single sheet of parchment and in the middle are traced
the words of a liturgical blessing in Latin. "The Lord
bless thee and keep thee, the Lord shew His face
unto thee and be merciful to thee, and turn His face
towards thee and grant thee peace." After the last
word, Francis put the letter "T"—his sign-manual,
and added "Brother Leo, the Lord bless thee" (*"Frater
Leo, Dominus benedicat te"*). Later, presumably
after Francis' death, Brother Leo added some notes
to the autograph. "Blessed Francis wrote this blessing
to me, Brother Leo, with his own hand," and below
the sign-manual—"in the same way he traced this sign
with his own hand." But at the very top of the sheet
Leo wrote the following lines in his own hand:

"Two years before his death, Blessed Francis kept Lent on Monte Verna (in honor of St. Michael, the Archangel) . . . and the hand of God was upon him by the vision of a seraph, and the impression of the stigmata upon his body." The earliest evidences, based on the eyewitnesses' record, describe the marks as "small excrescences resembling the marks of nails both in shape and color." Not till very much later would undisciplined piety turn those marks into "gaping wounds." It is a fact that from that time on Francis kept his hands hidden in the sleeves of his tunic and rode a donkey since walking became too hard for him.

The four friars stayed on Monte Verna for more than a fortnight. Not until September 30 were they able to leave for Portiuncula, a friend having arranged for Francis to be mounted throughout the whole journey. Before leaving, he took an affectionate farewell of the landscape, marking rocks, trees, and waters with a grateful glance. Nor did he forget the faithful falcon.

Through more than seven centuries the episode has undergone most varied treatment. Some among Francis' contemporaries, including a few German bishops, rejected it out of hand, but such rejection, born as it was of blind jealousy, meant little. Conversely, the record has suffered much at the hands of uncontrolled piety which, not satisfied with the genuinely miraculous element, exerted itself to force the incident into the reaches of the fantastic. Such piety seldom pauses to reflect that the genuine manifestations of the supranatural have simplicity for their basis.

But criticism, not always engendered by skepticism, was, and still is, voluminous. There is no scope here for more than one analysis of such an approach which is fatally easy to accept even by those who are neither atheists nor agnostics. It rests on apparently cogent arguments.

Here is a life crowded by inconceivable hardships and spent in a climate of an abnormally heightened religious consciousness. Here is an exhausted body, its weariness accentuated by several ailments, and a mind continually occupied with the supra-natural and, as frequently, a prey to anguish and a well-nigh pathological diffidence. Here, also, is a prolonged and intense preparation for every mental tissue to be wholly absorbed by all the details of the Passion. In somewhat narrowed terms, here is a long fast and a night spent in the expectation of what? A portent? An assurance? Most probably a vision. Given all that, what wonder that Francis' hold on the reality perceived by the senses should have been loosened, and that he believed in seeing what he could never have seen and feeling what he could never have felt. Under such circumstances even a controlled imagination might have leaped to a point where an entire angelic host could be seen riding the clouds, and how, those critics asked, could Francis' imagination have been controlled? As to the visible marks imprinted on his body, the phenomenon could well have originated out of the absorption in the Passion.

Such criticism has certainly a case, but it does fail because its arguments are based on a fragment and not the whole.

That night-long vigil on Monte Verna is but a detail, however stupendous, and it can be understood

only if considered within its context. The latter is
not an isolated sublime incident but Francis' truth
observed clearly enough since the day of his conversion, his whole life with its undeniably grotesque
touches, the same life which was spent not only in
tears over the world's trespasses but in laughter and
delight at the world's beauty, the life spent in conviction that the love of God was a simplicity and a
necessity. Francis was no philosopher but as a prince
among mystics he saw Time through the lens of
Eternity, and things created never ceased to mirror
the uncreaturely to him. Within that context, Monte
Verna may be considered both as an end and a beginning. It was the culmination of a mystic's striv-
ing, and the beginning of a stupendous adventure
not to cease with Francis' death. That mountain peak
in Italy typified a height accessible to anyone of faith
and good will. Just as Francis himself belongs to all
ages and all races, so his deepest experience is share-
able with those willing and able to contain it.

The matchlessly restrained language of Brother
Leo clothes the incident with a majesty no later chronicler ever captured. So much is told in so few lines to
explain the experience—insofar as any such experiences are explicable and communicable. A true
miracle does not interfere with the natural law but
does enhance it in a supra-natural way so far as man
is concerned, because there must be laws beyond his
capacity to understand. Few, if any, journeys made
by the spirit can be mapped out by the efforts of
matter. Within all such experience, the incommunicable heart abides where human language might be
likened to a wooden clapper trying to vie with a

Brahms Symphony. Here, the clamor of "Why" and "How" loses its meaning. Here lies the reality of the stigmata, the outward sign of Francis' union with his God.

One more point deserves consideration. Are not the very surroundings and the solemn climax somewhat of a contradiction when studied side by side with what was known of Francis? The shadowy cave, great cleft rocks to the right and the left, chasms and ravines, and long weeks spent in contemplating the most somber pages of the Gospels; and be it remembered that to the medieval people the physical aspects of the Passion carried infinitely more immediacy than they do to most Christians today.

Such is the background of Monte Verna—apparently hard to reconcile with a man who had formed a happy fellowship, insisted on cheerfulness, delighted in the least evidence of color and light, and never tired of reminding people about "the joy of the Lord."

But the contradiction is only apparent. However little he was able to tell the friars about the experience, his words contained a key. The imprinting of the stigmata was an agony—at once followed by joy. On Monte Verna, Francis was permitted to see both Gethsemane and Golgotha bathed in the light of the Easter morning.

CHAPTER ELEVEN

THE HOMECOMING

NO sooner had the four friars reached the borders of Umbria than their homecoming became something of a Roman triumph in little because the news of their approach had fired the whole countryside. Market stalls and shops were deserted, and even urgent field-work came to be forgotten. Excited crowds of men, women, and children took to milling up and down any road where they hoped they might be rewarded by a glimpse of Francis. They carried bread, cheese, fruit, and wine. On seeing the friars in the distance, the people started shouting their welcome, the reiterated "*Il Santo, il Santo*," troubling the little man and making his companions blush in confusion. But there was no silencing the people who knew that Francis' touch could and did heal and that his prayers never failed to win an answer from God.

The whole of Umbria knew that *il Poverello* had spent a long time in retreat. They knew no more than that except that it was good to have him back again. They gazed at him with pride and affection blended rather obviously with possessiveness.

There was a reason for the latter. For a long time, the common folk had considered Francis as a man singularly honored by God, the Virgin, and the saints, to whose intimate company their devotion had already admitted him. But was he not equally one of themselves, bred on the Umbrian soil, well acquainted

with Umbrian sunrises and sunsets, familiar with
every curve and coil of the daily life led in the country? Had death overtaken Francis in the valley on the
way to Portiuncula, the Assisians would have come
in their thousands to claim his body. They would
never have surrendered it to the Perugians, let alone
anyone further afield. In their eyes, Francis' fame rose
far higher than any of their own mountain peaks.
Assisi and no other town had a lien on him, the
people being already aware that he would never
wholly die in his death and that his shrine would
attract pilgrims down all the years to come.

So frail did Francis look that the possibility of
some such climax could not have been distant from
the minds of his companions. The return journey
from Monte Verna must have exhausted him to the
utmost, even though the three friars would take care
to leave the road at nightfall and to look for some
sheltered and secluded spot where they might spend
the night—no stranger's intrusion disturbing their
quiet.

All his weakness and pain notwithstanding, Francis rode down into the valley without denying himself to the people. His smile cheered them, his blessing comforted them. His touch had brought healing
before and did so again. What few words he spoke
were charged with a quiet joy and perfect serenity,
and the people knew that in his turn he was glad to
be back among them.

Portiuncula was reached at last. A little later the
most loyal of the brethren were told by Leo and
Angelo about Monte Verna. They were charged to
keep silent, but it is doubtful if the matter could

have remained private for long. Francis' obvious
lameness might indeed have been explained by his
general weakness and the intensified pain in his legs—
not so the hands now always kept hidden in the sleeves
of the tunic. Moreover, the wound in Francis' left
side bled a little from time to time.

Friars and lay friends alike noted a change in
him. His deepened serenity awed them. It bore the
quality of a newness just as though he had returned
to them from a world they had never seen. Again,
Francis now remained in his cell for long spells at a
time, and Brother Leo and others soon guessed that
solitude had become a necessity for their Father.

A brief rest at Portiuncula restored Francis'
strength and eased some of his many ailments. The
blinding headaches grew less frequent, and the pain
in his eyes was not as sharp as it had been. A visit
to San Damiano refreshed him much. It would be
no idle conjecture to think that to Clare, and Clare
alone, could he tell details of his experience he would
not have shared with anyone else.

By November Francis felt that he must be about
his business again. Together with three friars, he
left Portiuncula on what was to prove his last missionary journey. He did not travel beyond Umbria,
however, and the little company passed from town
to town, from hamlet to hamlet, by laboriously slow
stages, Francis always riding a donkey. He allowed
his friends to persuade him that his wasted body
needed a greater protection than the rough brown
tunic could afford, and he wore a warmer garment
underneath. He also gave up the rigors of fasting.

Now his sermons were briefer than ever. On occasions his weakness forbade him to utter more

than a few sentences. "Love God. . . . Remember that
Jesus redeemed you. . . . Revere His altars where He
gives you Himself. . . . Learn His peace and let it
possess your hearts. . . . Never covet, . . . Forgive
those who hurt you and win your enemy's friendship.
. . . Turn away from sin. . . . Praise God for the world
He has made. . . ."

There was nothing intrinsically new in any of it,
but the spirit which prompted those simplicities to
be spoken was charged with a freshness seldom if
ever heard in the speech of that day, and the people
who listened to Francis were able to grasp that in-
vigorating quality, however poor their own articulacy.
As so often before, they realized that they were listening to a man who had lived the truths he spoke
about, to whom God's love, peace, and joy were
realities as simple as air, earth, and water. As so
often before, many among the hearers made their
answer, each in his or her way, by reconciliations,
unaccustomed gestures of charity, a less jaundiced
approach to the day's hard rub, a deepened apprecia-
tion of all the beauty they saw about them.

That last missionary journey brought much joy
to Francis. But, in spite of many halts made for his
rest in rewarding seclusion, the effort ended by proving too much for his shredded strength. His eyesight
grew steadily worse. His legs began to swell, and
his companions were horrified by the first of many
hemorrhages. What medical help could be found in
the neighborhood brought hardly any relief to Francis.
But he did not complain. "Brother Ass, Brother Ass,"
he would say to his wasted body. "You think your
work is quite finished. I know it is not."

On Christmas Eve 1224, Francis and his com-

panions came to Poggio-Buscone, a hamlet on the
way to Rieti, where a great crowd was waiting to
welcome him. His eyesight so poor that he was
scarcely able to tell one face from another, Francis
said to the people:

"Here you have come expecting to see a saint, and
where is he? My friends, I am a sinner. Why, I have
not even kept a proper Advent—I have been dining
off meat every day."

Christmas over, Francis and his little company
began thinking of their return to Portiuncula when
a messenger from Cardinal Ugolino came to see them.

A revolt having driven Honorius III from Rome,
the Papal court was at Rieti all through the winter
of 1224–5. Both the Pope and the Cardinal were
distressed when they heard about Francis' continual
trouble with his eyes. A famous physician was then
in attendance on the Pope, and Ugolino wrote that
Francis must come to Rieti and receive proper treatment.

Brother Leo and the other friars were overjoyed.
They used all their persuasion to win Francis' consent, but they failed. The little man dictated a note
of courteous thanks to the Cardinal saying that he
did not think any physician in the world could help
him because the trouble with his eyes had gone too
far.

There was yet another reason for refusing the
invitation.

The radiance of that September dawn on Monte
Verna now stayed close to Francis, and again receded, as was but natural. His hours of solitude were
more a necessity than ever. He could neither preach

nor counsel as much as he used to. Often enough, during the lonely spells, or even when together with his companions, Francis' old demon would attack him and shroud his mind with doubt and anxiety for the future. Such moods, all but brushing against despair, would, so he thought, be intensified if he were to find himself once again at the Papal court, with its turbulent climate of jealousy, intrigue, and wearying conversation. He had laid down his authority. There was no longer any need for him to meet any ecclesiastical officials. What had he, God's beggar that he was, to do with courts? He had neither desire nor strength to engage in verbal battles with men whose arguments he had not been able to follow clearly even in his days of good health.

Such were the motives behind Francis' decision at Christmas 1224. But, once the winter and spring were over, he changed his mind. In July 1225 he dictated two messages, one to Clare at San Damiano and the other to the Cardinal. He told Clare that he would be coming to San Damiano "for a few days' rest." He told Ugolino that he would make for Rieti on leaving the Poor Clares.

There is nothing to tell us about the reasons for this decision. It may well have been due to the importunity of the loyal friars now more anxious than ever that their Father should not neglect an opportunity to avail himself of the highest medical skill in the whole of Italy. Yet, of all the likely conjectures, Clare's persuasion would have carried most weight with Francis.

She and her sisters were overjoyed when they heard that he was coming to them. With their own

hands they built a small hut of reeds and tree
branches in a secluded corner of their garden, with
olives, tamarisks, and umbrella pines in the background, and a stream running close by. The sisters
were determined to surround Francis with every
comfort. They meant to ward off any unwarrantable
and irksome intrusion from the outside, to cosset him
as much as he would permit and, the brief rest over,
to send him off to the care of the famous man at Rieti,
their prayers to companion him all along the way.

It was mid-July when Francis came to San Damiano for a few days—he would not leave for Rieti
until September.

As usual, it refreshed him to see his great friend,
but he came to her exhausted in mind far more than
in body.

He was Father and Founder of the vast Franciscan
family. His sons were now all over Germany, Spain,
and France, and had begun their work in the Low
Countries and in England. For all the cleft in their
ranks, both Conventuals and Strict Observants regarded him with equal veneration, but Francis felt
torn in two between the opposing camps. All his
courtesy and charity notwithstanding, he would look
at a Conventual wearing the same rough brown tunic
and then think of the vast and complicated organization of which the friar was a member, as an immense
cobweb spun over all the simplicities of the earlier
days. Francis felt that he should have prevented it
all. He should never have acquiesced in the adoption
of the 1223 Rule.

"They have taken away my family," he once said
to Clare, "and it is all my fault."

For many years he had sustained her. Now she knew that her own turn had come. She comforted, she encouraged, and she prayed harder than ever. A feebler faith than hers would have been shattered, but she stood firm.

At first, the sisters tried to nurse Francis, but all the soothing ointments they used for his eyes could not bring him any easement because, as a contemporary says, "He wept so much." Francis wept for the past which, as he then thought, should have been different, and for the future which—in his opinion—was but a womb carrying still sharper anguish. He had spent so many years in contemplating Eternity. Now, at San Damiano, a sick and disillusioned man, he seemed to become a gyved prisoner within calendared Time. He would tell his friends that he had no wish to hear anything concerning the Order and then start questioning them as to what was happening in Italy and beyond, although much of what they were able to tell him was but another thrust of a knife into a gaping wound.

Presently Francis' moods grew so darkly shrouded that he would see no one, not even Clare. Now the pure air of Monte Verna and its splendors were as though they had never been. He was in a wilderness, its skies unlit by a single star. Again he descended into a narrow valley, thick dust swirling up and down its reaches, and his very solitude provided refuge for horrors. His silence unbroken, Francis stayed in the little hut, and not even Brother Leo dared to disturb him.

But one morning the sisters at their work and the few friars who had followed Francis to San Damiano

heard soft singing from the direction of the hut. The
voice rang low and it halted occasionally, although it
sounded pure and sweet. Brother Leo and another
came nearer and waited, hoping for a call. It did
not come. But the next day the singing continued.
Presently, it broke off and after a pause came a call,
and Brother Leo went in to find Francis groping his
way to the entrance. The wasted face, upturned to
the skies he could hardly see, was the face of a man
who had been listening, and was still tranced by
what he had heard.

That day Francis asked for food, adding that he
would like to eat his dinner in the sisters' little refectory. They helped him across the garden, and had
him settled at the table when suddenly he turned his
face to the opened door and broke out singing:

Laudato sio lo Signore. . . .

The sisters, bowls of beans in their hands, stopped
serving. The friars present raised their heads, amazement and joy in their eyes. The sweet clear voice
went on. The first line was followed by another, a
third, and a fourth. Then Francis paused. A robin
was pecking at some crumbs scattered outside the
open door. He could not see the bird, but a smile
broke on his face. Leaning slightly forward, he sang
the four lines again:

Almighty, highest, good Lord,
Thine are all praise and glory and honor and
    blessing,
To Thee alone, All-highest, all things belong,
And who among us is worthy to speak Thy
    Name?

There followed another pause. Someone stirred
and went to fetch paper and an inkhorn. Then the
clear voice rang again with the joy and vigor of
earlier years. Verse upon verse, the whole creation
was knit together in a paean of praise and gratitude,
beginning "very specially (*spetialmente*) with the
Brother Sun," whose splendor reflected the glory of
God. The theme swept through the stellar world and
winged down to the earth. Air, wind, clouds, and
weather, "*onne tempo*," whether kind or unkind, were
all invited to enter the gates of praise, and they were
joined by "the humble, chaste, and precious sister
water" and "brother fire, by whose power darkness
was vanquished, brother fire, so beautiful and merry
and strong . . . (*e bello et jucundo et robustoso* . . .)."
Finally, the Lord was to be praised for "our sister
and mother earth . . . producing varied fruits and
colored flowers and grasses. . . . (*et produci diversi
fructi con colorite flori et herba* . . .)."

The *Canticle of the Sun* may be taken as a poet's
preface to Francis' great Testament so soon to be
written, an artist's interpretation of the truth lived in
through many years and, finally, as a lover's passionate homage paid in recognition of all the beauty
received at the hands of the Beloved. Francis sang
of nature as he had known it in his native Umbria,
but the praise of the mother earth and the elements
included the whole world. He would never know it,
but by his last poetic flight he became a brother to
all mankind down the centuries to come. The Canticle
was no outburst of a passing lyrical impulse but the
flower of several happily unclouded moments, its
petals unlikely to shrivel and fade at the approach of
a shadow in the mind.

Francis had found his way back—not to lose it
again—into the condition where, the finite betrothed
to the infinite—an inheritance not his alone but common to all of good faith—became assured. He had
reached the point where, still within Time, he could
comprehend Eternity.

Now all untoward circumstances of the past were
swept out of his consciousness. Once again, Francis
could truly acknowledge himself *"joculator Domini,"*
the song on his lips at one with the song in his heart.
Once again he knew himself to be a knight of the
Lord and a liegeman of the Lady Poverty, in however
odd a guise his contemporaries chose to see her.

Brother Leo and all the other friars who were at
San Damiano at once learned the Canticle by heart,
and they sang it as they went about their work. Singing those lines, they set out for Rieti in the following
September, with the sisters' prayers for their comfort
and refreshment. Their way led through one of the
loveliest corners of Europe, all along the whimsical
course of the Velino. *"Laudato sio lo Signore. . . ."*
The echoes kept rising and falling under the deep
blue Umbrian skies.

They had indeed learned all the verses by heart,
but the poem stood for far more than words could
convey. To dedicated men like Brothers Egidio, Bernardo, Masseo, Rufino, Angelo, Illuminato and, most
particularly, Brother Leo, the Canticle was at once a
clarion call, a great affirmation, and also a source of
joy because the poet in the Founder had broken his
long silence. The friars felt that all the hard, and
sometimes heartbreaking, but also exciting and de-
lightful labors of the years were gathered up in those

stanzas. As they sang them, they learned once again that, whether preaching or toiling with their hands in a vineyard or a pigsty, they and the whole creation were at one in praising the Creator.

Francis had come to Rieti for treatment. To his immediate relief, he found that his earlier anxieties had been groundless. Neither the Cardinal nor any other prelate came to weary him with administrative problems or theological arguments. Ugolino's welcome was warm and compassionate, and he had Francis lodged in comfort. The great physician and his colleagues were most assiduous in their desire to cure *il Poverello*. No known remedy, however rare or costly, was spared to heal his various ailments. There were unguents for his eyes, cordials to allay his digestive trouble, special herbal distillations for his swollen limbs, and some of the disorders began responding to the treatment.

But not the sight. Francis was no longer able to read, and the sharp morning sun must now be screened from him. All the remedies having failed, the physicians held a council. One means alone remained: cautery.

At the sight of the brazier being brought in, the friars present shuddered with horror and hurried out of the room. Francis' own mouth shook a little. Then he stretched out his hands toward the flame and said: "Brother fire, I have always loved you. Please be kind to me now," and he submitted to the excruciating operation without a murmur. When it was over, his companions came back into the room, and Francis gently chided them for their pusillanimity.

The cautery, however, did not restore his sight.

It was later followed by another equally futile and painful operation. In the end, the physicians had to tell Cardinal Ugolino and Brother Elias, the Minister-General of the Order, that all their remedies were exhausted. Now Francis was virtually blind and, as was only to be expected, the two operations had greatly increased his weakness. He was eager to leave Rieti, but the Cardinal wondered if the little man would survive the return journey to Assisi.

"But I must go back where I belong, my lord," Francis said firmly.

Yet they could not return at once. Francis' condition began worsening from day to day, and one date after another had to be canceled. In the end it was not till the spring of 1226 that the friars were able to leave Rieti, and a most studiedly circuitous route had to be planned in order to avoid passing through any town or hamlet along the way since the least exertion would have been fatal to Francis. Nor could he ride any longer. Leo, Masseo, Rufino, and Angelo carried the litter in turns. It greatly grieved them that they were going to Assisi and not to Portiuncula, but Francis was an Assisian, his death was expected almost daily, and the city longed to have him back within its walls. On that occasion he and the other friars were lodged in Bishop Guido's palace.

They had fully expected Francis to die almost immediately on their return. To assure the greatest quiet possible to the sick man, the palace was surrounded by guards and none but friars were permitted to see him. To everybody's surprise, however, Francis rallied within a few days.

There was still some work left for him to do, he told his friends. Preaching was now beyond him, but he owed it to all not to be idle. So he summoned what little strength remained to him and started dictating his very last messages to Leo and Rufino in turn. The work proceeded at a snail's pace. In the first place, Francis weighed every word most carefully. Secondly, exhaustion would gain on him after two or three sentences had been spoken. But he refused to give up.

His first thought was of Clare. An enclosed nun, she could not come to him, and Francis knew he would never see San Damiano again. By 1226, several houses of Poor Clares had had the Benedictine Rule imposed on them to the great grief of the Foundress. At San Damiano, however, the Lady Poverty still walked about, her lovely feet unshod, and Clare's loyalty all down the years had greatly sustained Francis. It is known that he composed a brief admonition to the sisters, for the last time encouraging them not to give up the original Rule and assuring them of his prayers. Unfortunately, no copy of it has been preserved.

Then there followed a letter addressed to the entire Franciscan Order, and most guardedly did Francis word it. "Keep nothing for yourselves that He may receive you without reserve, Who has given Himself to you without reserve. . . ." There was also a message to "all the Christians in the world." It did not mention the Tertiaries as such but its contents rather suggest that Francis had their welfare very much in his mind when composing the epistle. "I, little brother Francis, being everybody's servant, must

serve all men. . . . Seeing that I am too ill and feeble
to visit any of you, I have decided to send you my
message. . . ." Once again, now for the last time, the
restatement of old truths came to be clothed with a
directness and a simplicity which had breathed
through every sermon preached by Francis. He belonged to God and to Eternity. He also belonged to
the world, and the care for that vast family would
not leave him until the end.

Finally, there was the longest and the most important document of all, which became known as Francis'
Testament. Together with the *Canticle of the Sun*,
it is the finest written memorial he left to the world.

In a certain sense, the Testament may be considered as an autobiographical fragment even though
its directly personal details are meagre enough and
are so interwoven with the vaster issues of his
calling as to lose the least subjective approach. Yet,
however few the personal details, the whole of Francis comes to life in them—his humility, which never
succumbed to the level of servility, his obstinacy, his
occasionally bizarre contradictions, and always his
serene consciousness of being right about his vocation.

When I led a sinful life in the world, it used
to be most painful to me even to look at a leper,
but God brought me into [their] midst, and I
remained [at the hospital] for some time. When
I left, all the hard and bitter things had become
sweet and easy. . . . When the Lord gave me
some brothers, nobody showed me (*"nemo ostendebat mihi"*) what I must do but the Most High
Himself revealed to me that we must live in

perfect accordance with the Gospels. . . . I
worked with my hands . . . [and] I desire most
firmly that all the friars should work at some
honorable trade. . . .

Once again, as so often before, Francis reaffirmed
his faith and his loyalty to the Church and her priest-
hood. "The Lord gave me (and He still gives) so
great a faith in priests . . . that even if they persecuted
me, I would have recourse to them. . . . I will not
consider their sins [but] their sacerdotal office
alone. . . ." Yet, as will shortly be shown, Francis'
deep-rooted reverence for the priestly office was determined by the fact of the clergy being dispensers of
sacramental grace. They consecrated the Host. They
alone had the power to absolve sins. Francis' devotion to the Blessed Sacrament plumbed depths but
rarely reached in his generation. The account of its
institution in the Upper Room was graven in his
memory, and the priestly office, he held most fervently,
alone could give God houseroom on God's altars.
The number of sadly neglected churches and chapels
in Italy alone goes a long way to prove that great
numbers of Francis' contemporaries were lukewarm
about those altars—except towards the evening of
their lives.

Veneration for the sacerdotal office and all, there
still remained vast reaches of the soul where even the
clergy could not enter. In the following sentences
Francis reaffirmed the principle he had defended from
his youth, the principle of a soul's ultimate liberty:
". . . not even the Pope may command you anything
contrary to the conscience or to the Rule. . . . In any

conflict, God's voice and one's conscience must be listened to and obeyed. . . ."

There followed paragraphs revealing the depth of the travail in Francis' soul when he fell to considering all that had happened to his family since a particular chapter when, his leadership laid down, those to whom his ideals could say nothing had begun introducing one innovation after another. At that time Francis had accepted all the changes. Now, with the breath of death almost upon his face, he decided to repudiate the acceptance and to speak with an authority of which no chapter could deprive him—the authority of a Founder.

> I absolutely forbid all the Brothers, wherever they should be, to ask for any Bull from the Court of Rome, whether directly or indirectly, or under the pretext of obtaining permission to preach. . . . Should [the friars] not be received at any place, let them go elsewhere, thus doing penance with the blessing of God. . . . Let [them] take great care not to receive churches or houses . . . except as all is in accord with the Holy Poverty which we have vowed to serve . . . and let [the brethren] not receive hospitality except as pilgrims and strangers. . . .

Then followed the most emphatic closing lines:

> Let not the Brothers say "This is a new Rule." . . . I am sending you a reminder and a warning. . . . It is my Will that I, little Brother Francis, make for you, my blessed Brothers, in order that we may less imperfectly observe the

Rule which we have promised to keep. . . . Let
the Ministers-General take nothing from or add
nothing to these words. When the Rule is read,
let these words be read also.

Francis' Testament was no appeal but rather a
signpost to a road so many among his sons had forsaken, although in one sentence after another the
cleft in the family was calmly ignored. He was in-
spired to write as the Founder and Guardian for all
time, never as an administrator whose authority and
functions would inevitably be governed by fugitive
circumstance. The Rule so frequently referred to is
not the 1223 variant solemnly confirmed by Pope
Honorius III, but the earliest pattern based on evangelical simplicities and the service of the Lady
Poverty. Side by side with Francis' rock-hewn profession of loyalty to the Church, we find his steadfast
and passionate conviction that God and one's conscience must stand above ecclesiastical rulings if a
particular crisis should demand it. Oddly enough,
there is no ambiguity in such an apparently irrecon-
cilable juxtaposition.

The Testament, dictated by Francis so slowly and
laboriously, was the fruit of his soul's hidden harvest.
The Franciscan sowing-time now lay behind, and
not for him to know that some of the seeds would
struggle into life at most unexpected moments and
in most unexpected places. He wrote the Testament
for the Order, almost every line informed not so
much by the anguish for the past as by the serenity
which possessed him at the end. Yet, written as it
was for the Franciscan family, the Testament had a

relevance for the entire Christian world. It has not lost any of its meaning down to our own day. It utters a challenge against all falsely colored piety, all spiritual gyves imposed on man, against shoddy compromise, and equally cheap expediency. One among the Popes, at least, would have accorded it his unqualified approval, Leo the Great, who said—in words which could never be matched—that to serve God was to reign in perfect freedom.

Alas, as was only to be expected, the Testament came not only to be ignored by the Conventuals but it led them to persecute the Strict Observants for the veneration they were courageous enough to pay to the last words of the Founder. To cite but two examples, Francis' first disciple, Bernardo di Quintavalle, had to go into hiding in the most remote regions of the Apennines to escape a probable death at the hands of the Conventuals. Another loyal adherent, a German friar, Caesar of Speyer, was imprisoned for daring to assert that he considered the Testament binding on his conscience. In that prison, Caesar was eventually murdered by the friar detailed to have him in his charge. Cells and hermitages known to shelter the Strict Observants were searched at the order of the Minister-General. Copies of the Testament were burned and their possessors imprisoned and manhandled most savagely. Finally, some four years after Francis' death, Cardinal Ugolino, then Pope Gregory IX, dealt at some length with the Testament in his bull *Quo Elongati*, and declared that the Brothers Minor were not bound to observe its precepts. Nothing but the heroic efforts of Francis' faithful sons preserved some copies of the manuscript for posterity.

The Testament finished, Francis knew his work was done. Brother Leo and others had feared that the effort of dictating so much would sap him to the utmost but, although very weary, he seemed slightly better, and he would not deny himself to many visitors who now daily crowded the Bishop's palace. Presently, a friend of Francis', a well-skilled doctor from Arezzo, came to Assisi. At his entering the room, the little man sent the friars away and put a blunt question to the visitor. "How much longer have I left?" The doctor took refuge in a threadbare ambiguity. That did not satisfy Francis. "Can you not tell me the truth?" Having examined him, the visitor said that God was all powerful. Francis understood and remained calm. "I am not a cuckoo to be afraid of death. By God's grace, it is no matter to me whether I live or die."

So the doctor told him that his ills were far beyond any physician's skill. "There is very little time left for you," he added.

Francis thanked his friend and wished him a comfortable journey back to Arezzo. The friars came back into the room and he broke the news to them. They began to weep but Francis instantly checked their sobs by singing a new verse of the *Canticle of the Sun*, the four lines composed by him immediately on hearing the doctor's verdict. "Praised be the Lord for our sister, the death of the body. . . ." At first, his companions stood and stared dumbly. Then they began repeating the words after Francis and, having learned them by heart, they sang the verse to the end, he joining them, a smile on his ravaged face.

Then one of the friars broke into the opening stanza, and they all took it up. They came to the end of the Canticle and started it all over again. The supper bell rang and they never heard it. A servant of the Bishop's came in with the food for Francis and was amazed to find them all singing. The man wondered if the Father were feeling better, and someone's reply, "He is about to go home," bewildered the man into silence. Darkness fell, and the friars were still singing. They were at it until dawn.

In the end, Bishop Guido's household was shocked by what they considered to be unpardonable levity. Brother Elias, the Minister-General, was then staying at Assisi, and he is said to have rebuked Francis. "We know, Father, that you are about to die, but death should be awaited with fear and trembling and not with joy." It is not known what reply Francis made to those words which rather painfully illustrate the depth of the cleavage in the Order.

However, the displeasure of the episcopal household made it all difficult for the friars. When Francis firmly said he wished to be taken to Portiuncula, nobody protested, and a litter was quickly prepared. His faithful sons carried him out of the city. On their way across the valley, just as they approached the ruined leper hospital, Francis asked them to stop and to turn the litter round. He could not see Assisi, but he knew he was facing it, and he gave it his last blessing.

Nor could he see Portiuncula when they reached it, but he breathed its pure air with evident relief. The few days left to him were radiant. "*Mortem cantando suscepit.*" "He accepted death—singing," so

Thomas of Celano would write, the truest epitaph to be bestowed on a poet.

During his last night Francis felt hungry. Some bread was brought in, and he had enough strength to break it and share it with the others. They went on singing Psalms and various canticles of the Office, but his own voice was too weak to join them. Dawn came, and the day passed serenely. All pain having gone, Francis lay very still, birdsong and his sons' voices for him to hear. With the first evening shadows, his breath was stilled.

The deep southern dark had already fallen when those who kept vigil in the little cell heard the singing of larks above the thatched roof.

A legend? Possibly, but at least a legend in perfect accord with Francis' truth.

CHAPTER TWELVE

ONE WORD MORE

THE majestic clauses of the Nicene Creed had lost none of their power in Francis' day. Christ, the Son of the Father, was the Second Person of the Blessed Trinity. He was enfleshed for man's salvation and died on the Cross for man's sin. He rose on the third day, thus fulfilling the prophecies about Him. He ascended into heaven, there to reign co-equal with the Father. He would come again to mete out His judgment to the living and the dead, and of His kingdom there would be no end. To Francis, all of it meant precisely what it meant to every Catholic of his generation, and today.

The Creed had to be accepted as the foundation of faith but, dogmas apart, there remained the liberty of building individual images of Christ, a liberty invariably respected so long as a particular image did not run counter to the canonical precepts. Some of these images—such as, for instance, the Light of the world and the Good Shepherd—were borrowed from the Gospels. Others sprang from a poet's imagination. Venantius Fortunatus' picture of Christ as the Lord of spring, His Resurrection echoed in breaking leaf and budding flower, may be cited as one such example.

Ailred of Rievaulx compared Christ with the keystone in the arch of true friendship.

The Scandinavians, latest newcomers to the Christian household, envisaged Him as an intrepid viking,

Who faced death, no thought of defeat in His mind,
and Whose Cross was a fortress:

> A stronghold ever shall I find
> Beneath His mantle purple-lined,
> There I my guilt will cover.

Something of the same staunch ruggedness found
its way into the medieval crucifixes of German workmanship.

Away from the paths of orthodoxy, one heresiarch
after another would occupy their imagination in building Christological images which often distorted dogma
and common sense together, and one council after
another sought to shatter those heresies.

Francis held fast to the Creed, but in the matter of
his vocation he owed nothing either to Church or to
schools, and he said so in words shorn of all
vanity because of their simplicity: *"Nemo ostendebat
mihi. . . ."* i.e., "Nobody showed me. . . ." A faithful
son of the Church, he revered the priestly office, and
never lost an opportunity of stressing the gulf between its sacramental meaning and the personal de-
merits and worse of the priests. Never ordained himself, Francis was, nonetheless, "a priest forever" since
the power of administering God's grace was undoubtedly his.

The reality of God was mirrored for him in all
creation as is shown by many evidences of reverence
he paid not only to his own kind, animals, birds, and
fishes but to trees, flowers, and stones. There are epi-
sodes in his life which remind one of a passage in
the Book of Genesis about Jacob and the stone at
Bethel—so specially inhabited by God. To Francis,

the Spirit of God was the source of all life in man
and in nature, but those who at the beginning were
so ready to accuse him of worshipping a beech or a
sprig of rosemary, ended by digging a pit under their
own feet. In spite of all these appearances, Francis
was neither animist nor pantheist but remained a
Catholic in the truest sense of the word.

What about his own image of Christ?

Long before his voyage to Palestine, Francis had
lived in Galilee—which to him was Umbria, part of
the same world where the Word made flesh still
dwelt among men. His manner of living in that country breathed of an intimacy which shocked many
among his contemporaries. Francis' Jesus was no
figure of an uncontrolled imagination. Down to the
smallest details, He was Jesus of the Gospels, Who
knew the use of a carpenter's tools, enjoyed a wedding, left His home to be about His Father's business,
took delight in wild flowers, had no pillow for His
head and no concern for the morrow. Who broke
bread in sinners' company, was acquainted with fear
and grief, and also did a few incomprehensible things
such as speaking rudely to His mother and cursing
a harmless fig tree. What Francis made of such inci-
dents we cannot tell, but the medieval satire known
as "The Gospel According to the Silver Mark" affords
enough proof of the reception such a Jesus would
have received at the gates of the Lateran.[1]

---

[1] The reference here is to an excerpt from a thirteenth-
century manuscript known as *Carmina Burana*, which was
kept at the monastery of Benediktbeuern in Bavaria. It is a
motley collection of songs, stories, parodies, and satires. Some
of the contents are pious, others starkly profane. It was first

That deeply evangelical background lay at the root
of Francis' intimacy with his Lord, wholly God and
wholly Man. He held that all those who believed in
Christ could have no greater joy than that of being
united to Him, which is the common goal of all
Christians, but Francis marched towards it with a
difference. He certainly belonged to his day, but he
was also an intimate of the past and a herald of the
future.

To begin with, he saw his way with a clarity
granted to very few. He walked it in such a manner
that he became a legend even in his lifetime. He was
an Arthur but he sought, and found, more than the
Holy Grail. He was also a Galahad and a de Bouillon,
thirsting to spend himself in God's service—not
merely for his own soul's salvation but that of many.
Here, Francis stands virtually alone in his generation
when men and women would immerse themselves in
pious practices primarily and all too often solely to
assure their own salvation.

Again, Francis' unfailing delight in the visible
world set him apart from his fellows. His reasoning
was simple enough: all things were God's gifts and

---

edited by J. A. Schmeller in 1847—"The Gospel According
to the Silver Mark" tells the story of a beggar coming to
the Lateran Palace to ask for help; the Cardinal would not
help him until he had some alms to give them. So he sold
what poor clothes he had and brought the money to the
Pope's palace, but the Cardinal said: "What is this among
so many?" and would not let him in. The poor man "wept
bitterly, as one that could not be comforted."

The excerpt can be found in G. G. Coulton's *Life in the
Middle Ages* (Cambridge: The University Press; 1928) Vol.
I, p. 112.

therefore sources of joy. He did not worship a stream when washing his feet in it but he thanked God for the purity of the water. He would cup his hands round some wild flower and see in its beauty the promise of a splendor as yet unseen. The medieval "vale of tears" was to him a valley of song. To mourn for one's sins was but one part of a man's landscape. Much more of it was bathed in light and joy.

No theologian, no pragmatist, no architect of communities, Francis succeeded in opening a wide window in the medieval house. He dared to call himself *"joculator Domini."* For all his frequent moods of sadness and anguish, he could laugh and sing until his death. And he possessed that rare gift of sharing which joins both giver and recipient in a bond of unshakable charity. He taught all those who came to him a new approach to any difficulty in their lives—from a bitter family feud to a tumbling down roof. Many people, having once heard him, would go on their way, aware that they could be bigger, better, and more courageous than they were. That gift of Francis' had a quality which still brings him close to your door and mine.

But he was born into a sharply checkered world, where time and again the thickening shadows suggested that all light stood in danger of being put out. Because Francis stood within a wholeness few had ever achieved, he did not keep himself aloof from the shadows.

They, as he believed, stemmed from evil, and evil to Francis was not a problem to ponder about, still less to analyze, but a fact to recognize, to struggle against and, finally, to conquer. Again, as he saw it, it was the outcome of the Fall, and the evidences of the

Devil at work were plentiful enough in his generation. Troubles of one kind or another were shaking the
whole of Europe. There were insidious heresies to
disturb the faith of simple people, and at least one of
them, that of the Cathari, threatened to destroy the
whole social structure of the day. Flails of pestilence,
famine, and civil war, to say nothing of brigandage,
descended mostly on those unregarded folk whose
only crime was their penury. One tumult after another
colored the Italian skies with angry red. The Emperor
Otto IV having been excommunicated by one Pope,
his successor was waging a war against Innocent
III's successor. The commercial health of some countries was good—but for the fortunate minority only.
The triple cancer of simony, graft, and immorality
was eating deep into the Church. The earlier enthusiasm of the crusading movement had turned to
sorry ashes, and chivalry's face was most ignobly
stained. Finally, insofar as Francis could understand
(and there he was grievously at fault as will be
shown), learned men spent their days and nights over
obscure speculative problems, their solution unlikely
to ease the misery of mankind.

To him, the sum total of it was the fruit of the
Devil's machinations and treacheries. Yet there always
remained the grace and the mercy of God, and the
little Umbrian was convinced that man made in God's
likeness could rise above circumstances—however
cruel—and above evil, also.

But Francis was no reformer. He had the power to
heal many of the hurts to the soul and the mind caused
by existing social conditions. He had neither the gift
nor the knowledge required for changing the condi-

tions. Still less was he an administrator, and that should not be imputed to him as a fault.

That small fellowship, so ardently dedicated to the service of the Lady Poverty, singing at their work in the neighborhood of Assisi and later throughout the length and breadth of Umbria, should not be seen as an image of the mustard seed. It is doubtful if Francis himself had envisaged the immense numbers of men who would flock to his banner—and that so suddenly and hurriedly. In the light not only of contemporary conditions but of human nature, the subsequent cleft in their ranks was inevitable. The exquisite lowliness, perfect simplicity, and radiance of San Damiano, Rivo-Torto, and Portiuncula could never have been maintained for long once the few became a crowd, a fact never really understood by Francis— not because of his obstinacy, though he possessed more than a fair share of it, but because of his simplicity.

Furthermore, Jesus Himself having told him what to include in the original Rule, Francis could not imagine why such coils of ecclesiastical red tape should ever have been wound around it. The cleavage in the brothers' ranks gave birth to mutual suspicion, lack of charity, a series of betrayals, and, finally, to violence. It all but broke the Founder's heart. A lesser man would have withdrawn himself altogether.

There remains one point where it is indeed possible to criticize him, and that is in his inexplicable attitude to learning.

Thomas of Celano records a singular prophecy spoken by Francis not long before his death. "The time will come when, their good name lost, the

brothers will be ashamed to shew themselves by day-
light," and the pages of the Heptameron, to cite but
one example, bear sad witness to the downfall of the
Order. But it was idleness and great possessions
which would cause the undoing, not learning. In
Paris and Oxford alone, the name of the Order came
to be synonymous with much splendor born of the
travail of the mind.

Sabatier was right to question the authenticity of
a note alleged to have been written by Francis to
Anthony of Padua. "It pleases me that you interpret
Holy Writ and theology in such a way . . . conformable to the Rule, that the spirit of prayer be
not extinguished either in you or in the others." Such
words were out of character where Francis was concerned. The note must have been faked some time
after his death to strengthen the case of the Conventuals in their attitude to academic labors of the
brethren.

Again, the note may well have been faked to
justify a particular paragraph in the Constitution, a
paragraph which would have been rejected out of
hand by the Founder: "We ordain that *nobody* [italics
mine] should be admitted into our Order unless they
be clerks well versed in grammar and logic, or such
laymen whose admission would serve to the greater
edification of clergy and people." *("Ordinamus quod*
nullus *recipiatur in ordine nostro nisi sit talis clericus
qui sit competenter instructus in grammatica vel
logica, aut nisi sit talis laicus de cujus ingressu est
valde celebris et aedificatio in populo et clero.")*

Here, the heavy hammer of ecclesiastical bureauc-
racy shattered to pieces the happy usage of the

Franciscan morning when nothing would be required of a man except his readiness to give all his possessions to the poor and to serve God in utter poverty, and that not for any "edification of people and clergy" but out of his love for God.

Francis' greatest mistake lay in admitting learned men into the fellowship and then refusing to let them continue with their studies. In all fairness, it should be said that the first scholars to be admitted were members of the University of Bologna who, having caught the fire from the missionaries sent out by Francis, became convinced that God called them to such a life. Francis welcomed those newcomers, and here we face another of his contradictions.

In the first place, those men should have been advised to join either the Benedictines or the Dominicans. All their ardor notwithstanding, the training they had had was such as to debar them from dedication to the ideals served by Francis. The mistake created a situation which would have its logical outcome after the cleavage when scholars were welcomed into the Franciscan Order because they were scholars.

Secondly, and even more significantly, it was strange to see a man of Francis' stature engaged in belittling one of the finest gifts of God to man. He lived in a day when mental horizons were being most wondrously enlarged and when the interest in the natural sciences began to oust the arid theological speculation from its pride of place at the universities. All of it remained an alien country to him, but it need not have been impossible for him to apply to that unknown region the words of the Creed—"by Whom all things were made, . . ." even though he did not consider it necessary for his sons to travel up and down its reaches.

Nonetheless, for all Francis' contradictions, he was never fragmented, and his very mistakes stem out of a simplicity which can silence all argument. From that quality came his genius to help the world of his day and for centuries to come. He was one of the very few enabled to weld grief and joy together, and to communicate the peace born of fusion.

His canonization four years after his death by Ugolino, then Pope Gregory IX, was certainly conformable to the hierarchic pattern. It was a liturgical necessity and a national anticlimax. The plain folk had enough vision to see that Francis, while still in the flesh, was at one with the company of those who, having followed the light to them accorded, know that when hope and faith have had their day, charity remains.

A NOTE ON BIBLIOGRAPHY

THE Franciscan canon is immense. A detailed bibliography can be found in the Oxford Dictionary of the Christian Church.

A great impetus to Franciscan studies was started by Paul Sabatier (1858–1928), whose biography of the Saint has—in a sense—never been superseded. It appeared in 1893, and the first English translation came out in 1898. Sabatier's "*Vie*" is the only modern book which has here been consulted. It should, however, be used cautiously. Sabatier's documentation could not be better. His interpretation of some facts, however, is colored by bias. The chief instance to be cited is his comment on the relationship between Cardinal Ugolino and St. Francis. Sabatier all but turns the Cardinal into an enemy of the Order and he makes no allowance for the fact that the Umbrian's original idea could never have been carried out in its entirety. The two men remained friends to the end.

In the first place, there are Francis' own writings. They are few in number, and all are short. There are scattered references in the primary sources which suggest that some of the pieces written by him have not survived. There is his Testament, a small book of Admonitions, a short piece on the Eucharist, a Rule for Hermits, seven letters, a paraphrase of the Lord's Prayer, and the *Canticle of the Sun*. The works were not put together until the seventeenth century, when L. Wadding of Antwerp, a member of the Order, edited them in 1623. They were first translated into English by an anonymous Franciscan in 1882.

The most important sources are the so-called "primary" biographies composed by men who knew Francis personally. They were written in the thirteenth century and have all been translated into English.

First come the two Lives by Thomas of Celano (c. 1190–1260). He joined Francis' company either in 1213 or 1214. The First Life was written at the instance of Pope Gregory IX in 1228, and the Second in 1247. The first English translation (by A. G. F. Howell) came out in 1908.

The Book of the Three Companions, e.g., Brothers Leo, Rufino, and Angelo, was written at Greccio in Umbria between 1236 and 1246. It does not aim at being a complete biography but it may well be put together with Francis' own writings, and it gives a most vivid portrait of the Saint. *The Book of the Three Companions* can justly be called the finest jewel of Franciscan literature.

The Mirror of Perfection was ascribed by Sabatier to Brother Leo, but the authorship has since been disputed. Sabatier was its first editor (1898). The first English translation appeared in 1908.

Among the later medieval biographies, St. Bonaventure's *Life* should be mentioned. Born in 1221, Bonaventure had no personal knowledge of the Saint. He wrote the book in 1263. The work is not wholly reliable. There are far too many exaggerations and accretions, and certain facts are brought into conformity with the official attitude of the day. The first English translation appeared in 1904.

The classic known as *The Little Flowers of St. Francis (Fioretti di San Francesco)* came to be written nearly a century after the Saint's death but much of it is based on reliable contemporary texts. It was first printed in Italy in 1476. An English translation came out in 1910. In broad terms, it is a collection of legends, but it depicts—with a wealth of authentic detail—the manner of life led by the first Franciscans. Few of the sayings attributed to Francis are genuine quotations and yet all of them accord with his character and his ideals.

INDEX

A NOTE ON THE TYPE

THE text of this book is set in Monticello, a Linotype revival of the original Binny & Ronaldson Roman No. 1, cut by Archibald Binny and cast in 1796 by that Philadelphia type foundry. The face was named Monticello in honor of its use in the monumental fifty-volume *Papers of Thomas Jefferson*, published by Princeton University Press. Monticello is a transitional type design, embodying certain features of Bulmer and Baskerville, but it is a distinguished face in its own right.

This book was composed, printed, and bound by The Haddon Craftsmen, Inc., Scranton, Pa. Typography and binding based on designs by W. A. Dwiggins.